TRIO

WRITING 2

The Intersection of Vocabulary, Grammar, & Writing

Alice Savage & Colin Ward

OXFORD

UNIVERSITY PRESS

OXFORD
UNIVERSITY PRESS

198 Madison Avenue
New York, NY 10016 USA

Great Clarendon Street, Oxford, ox2 6dp, United Kingdom

Oxford University Press is a department of the University of Oxford.
It furthers the University's objective of excellence in research, scholarship,
and education by publishing worldwide. Oxford is a registered trade
mark of Oxford University Press in the UK and in certain other countries

Director, ELT New York: Laura Pearson

Head of Adult, ELT New York: Stephanie Karras

Publisher: Sharon Sargent

Managing Editor: Tracey Gibbins

Senior Development Editor: Anna Norris

Executive Art and Design Manager: Maj-Britt Hagsted

Content Production Manager: Julie Armstrong

Design Project Manager: Lisa Donovan

Image Manager: Trisha Masterson

Senior Image Editor: Fran Newman

Production Coordinator: Christopher Espejo

ISBN: 978 0 19 485411 5 Student Book 2 with Online Practice Pack
ISBN: 978 0 19 485412 2 Student Book 2 as pack component
ISBN: 978 0 19 485413 9 Online Practice website

Printed in China

This book is printed on paper from certified and well-managed sources

ACKNOWLEDGEMENTS

Cover Design: Yin Ling Wong

Illustrations by: Ben Hasler, pg. 32, 58, 82, 108; Joseph Taylor, pg. 20, 44, 46, 70, 96, 120.

We would also like to thank the following for permission to reproduce the following photographs: pg. x N.Sritawat/Shutterstock, Takashi Images/Shutterstock; pg. 1 iStock/Ammentorp Photography, Bob Rowan/Progressive Image/Corbis, andresr/ iStock; pg. 4 Steve Hix/Somos Images/Corbis, jian wan/iStock, Izabela Habur/ iStock, Jutta Klee/Corbis, imging/Shutterstock, Anna Jedynak/Shutterstock; pg. 5 MBI/Alamy, Andy Dean Photography/Shutterstock, Hero Images/Corbis, andresr/iStock, mikkelwilliam/iStock; pg. 6 Konstantin Chagin/Shutterstock, Alex I. Forsey/Corbis, Scott Rothstein/Shutterstock, Westend61 GmbH/Alamy; pg. 7 Monkey Business Images/Shutterstock, Tetra Images/Corbis, DAJ/Getty Images, Robert Kneschke/Alamy, Topic Photo Agency/Corbis, Stewart Cohen/ Blend Images/Corbis; pg. 9 Chris Howes/Wild Places Photography/Alamy, GQ/Shutterstock, moodboard/Corbis, Carmine Salvatore/iStock, OJO Images Ltd/Alamy, Bubbles Photolibrary/Alamy, MaxyM/Shutterstock, Ammentorp Photography/iStock; pg. 19 Ariel Skelley/Blend Images/Corbi, Ariel Skelly/Getty Images, Aldo Murillo/Getty Images; pg. 21 Snezana Ignjatovic/Shutterstock, JGI/ Tom Grill/Blend Images/Corbis, William Perugini/Shutterstock, BFG Images/Getty Images, brians101/iStock, Beau Lark/Corbis; pg. 22 iStock/© amriphoto, Dennis MacDonald/age footstock; pg. 33 Mark Edward Atkinson/Blend Images/Corbis, ACE STOCK LIMITED/Alamy, Tim Pannell/Tetra Images/Corbis, leungchopan/ Shutterstock, YanLev/Shutterstock, Steve Debenport/iStock; pg. 45 Prestige/Getty Images, Jason Dewey/Getty Images, LuVo/iStock, igor.stevanovic/Shutterstock,

Brand New Images/Getty Images, Lane Oatey/Blue Jean Images/Getty Images; pg. 57 Jeff Morgan 08/Alamy, nicholashan/iStock, Stacy Walsh Rosenstock/ Alamy; pg. 59 Photo Patricia White 3/Alamy, Giorgio Magini/iStock, format4/ Alamy, Olesia Bilkei/Shutterstock, stefanolunardi/Shutterstock, Juanmonino/ iStock, IgorGolovniov/Shutterstock, Superstock/Getty Images; pg. 71 Christian Knospe/Shutterstock, Yellow Dog Productions/Getty Images, Sage78/iStock, Jaochainoi/Shutterstock, Jaochainoi/Shutterstock, Billy Hustace/Corbis; pg. 80 Peter Scholey/Alamy, tristan tan/Shutterstock; pg. 83 Jose Fuste Raga/Corbis, epa european pressphoto agency b.v./Alamy, Alexey Seleznev/Shutterstock, Randy Pench/MCT/Newscom, Paz Ruiz Luque/Getty Images, Fabrice Lerouge/ Onoky/Corbis; pg. 84 Volodymyr Burdiak/Shutterstock, neelsky/Shutterstock; pg. 95 Kevin Dodge/Corbis, Kali Nine LLC/iStock, REUTERS/Yves Herman YH/ ABP; pg. 97 avian75/iStock, Radius Images/Corbis, Jamie Grill/Corbis, MaxyM/ Shutterstock, Peter Adams/JAI/Corbis, Alin Brotea/Shutterstock; pg. 109 Maximilian Weinzierl/Alamy, holbox/Shutterstock, Phil Sills Photography/ Getty Images, Vector House/Shutterstock, Tom Wang/Alamy, iStock/svetikd/ Getty Images; pg. 121 Alex Segre/Alamy, Universal ImagesGroup/Getty Images, Steve Debenport/iStock, imageBROKER/Alamy, Photographers Choice/ Getty Images, syolacan/iStock; pg. 122 George Philipas/Alamy, FLPA/Wayne Hutchinson–www.agefotostock.com.

REVIEWERS

We would like to acknowledge the following individuals for their input during the development of the series:

Aubrey Adrianson
Ferris State University
U.S.A.

Sedat Akayoglu
Middle East Technical University
Turkey

Lisa Alton
University of Alberta
Canada

Türkan Aydin
Çanakkale Onsekiz Mart University
Turkey

Pelin Tekinalp Cakmak
Marmara University, School of Foreign
Languages
Turkey

Karen E. Caldwell
Zayed University
U.A.E.

Danielle Chircop
Kaplan International English
U.S.A.

Jennifer Chung
Gwangju ECC
South Korea

Elaine Cockerham
Higher College of Technology
Oman

Abdullah Coskun
Abant Izzet Baysal University
Turkey

Linda Crocker
University of Kentucky
U.S.A.

Adem Onur Fedai
Fatih University Preparatory School
Turkey

Greg Holloway
Kyushu Institute of Technology
Japan

Elizabeth Houtrow
Soongsil University
South Korea

Shu-Chen Huang
National Chengchi University
Taipei City

Ece Selva Küçükoğlu
METU School of Foreign Languages
Turkey

Margaret Martin
Xavier University
U.S.A.

Murray McMahon
University of Alberta
Canada

**Shaker Ali Mohammed
Al-Mohammadi**
Buraimi University College
Oman

Eileen O'Brien
Khalifa University of Science,
Technology and Research
U.A.E.

Fernanda Ortiz
Center for English as a Second
Language at University of Arizona
U.S.A.

Ebru Osborne
Yildiz Technical University
Turkey

Joshua Pangborn
Kaplan International
U.S.A.

Erkan Kadir Şimşek
Akdeniz University Manavgat
Vocational College
Turkey

Veronica Struck
Sussex County Community College
U.S.A.

Clair Taylor
Gifu Shotoku Gakuen University
Japan

Melody Traylor
Higher Colleges of Technology
U.A.E.

Sabiha Tunc
Baskent University English Language
Department
Turkey

John Vogels
Dubai Men's College
U.A.E.

Author Acknowledgments

We would like to thank the many people who were involved in the development of *Trio Writing*, which began over Mexican food in Houston, where the idea for it was born in a meeting with Sharon Sargent, our friend and guide throughout this long process. Sharon, thank you for believing in us.

We are indebted to our brilliant editorial team: Tracey Gibbins, Mariel DeKranis, Keyana Shaw, Karin Kipp, and Anita Raducanu. We'd also like to give a special thanks to Stephanie Karras, who has been instrumental in bringing the idea to fruition.

Finally, we'd like to thank our friends and families, Margi Wald for sharing ideas and resources, our spouses Stefanie and Masoud who good-naturedly endured the endless beep of text messages as we sent ideas back and forth, and our children who made their own snacks when we were on a roll. It has been a wonderful journey, and we are very grateful to have had such fantastic fellow travelers.

—A. S. and C. W.

CONTENTS

Welcome to Trio Writing

Building Better Writers...From the Beginning

Trio Writing includes three levels of Student Books, Online Practice, and Teacher Support.

Level 1/CEFR A1

Level 2/CEFR A2

Level 3/CEFR B1

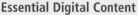

Essential Digital Content

iTools DVD-ROM with Classroom Resources

Trio Writing weaves together contextualized vocabulary words, grammar skills, and writing strategies to provide students with the tools they need for successful academic writing at the earliest stages of language acquisition.

Vocabulary Based On the Oxford 2000 🔑 Keywords

Trio Writing's vocabulary is based on the 2,000 most important and useful words to learn at the early stages of language learning, making content approachable for low-level learners.

Explicit, Contextualized Skills Instruction

Contextualized Grammar Notes and Writing Strategies are presented to teach the most useful and relevant skills students need to achieve success in their writing.

Readiness Unit

For added flexibility, each level of *Trio Writing* begins with an optional Readiness Unit to provide fundamental English tools for beginning students.

INSIDE EACH CHAPTER

▲ VOCABULARY

Theme-based chapters set a context for learning.

Essential, explicit skills help beginning learners to generate independent academic writing.

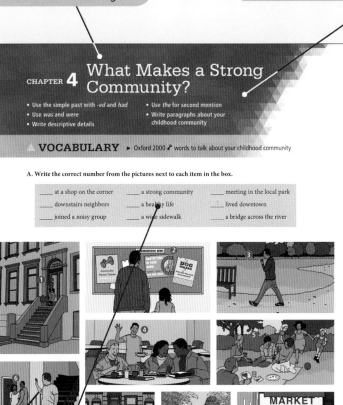

Vocabulary is introduced as a set of contextualized phrases built from the Oxford 2000 list of keywords to help students understand words in real contexts.

Vocabulary activities allow for abundant mixing and matching, giving students new ways to assemble words and multiword units.

Trio Writing Online Practice extends learning beyond the classroom, providing students with additional practice and support for each chapter's vocabulary, grammar, and writing instruction.

▲▲ GRAMMAR

A two-part grammar presentation with sentence-building practice recycles key vocabulary.

Achievable writing models provide examples of grammar skills in the context of each chapter's writing assignment.

Each grammar lesson contains two Grammar Notes, which are matched closely to the writing task for supportive grammar instruction.

Sentence-building charts provide structure while allowing students options to generate independent writing.

Vocabulary and Grammar Chants found online help students internalize the target grammar structure and vocabulary for greater accuracy and fluency when writing.

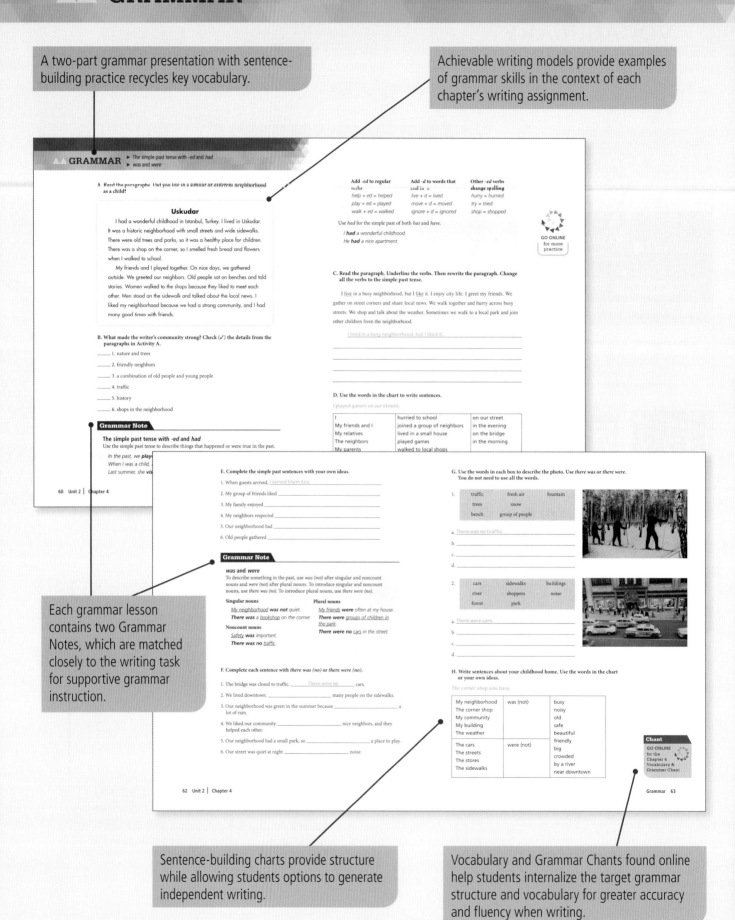

▲▲▲ WRITING

After providing practice with a variety of sentence types, *Trio Writing* guides students to generate meaning within and across sentences in the form of a longer writing task.

The Writing lesson builds on the first two lessons by bringing the language and theme together in a six-step, scaffolded writing task. Even the earliest-level language learners are able to create a portfolio of academic writing with *Trio Writing*.

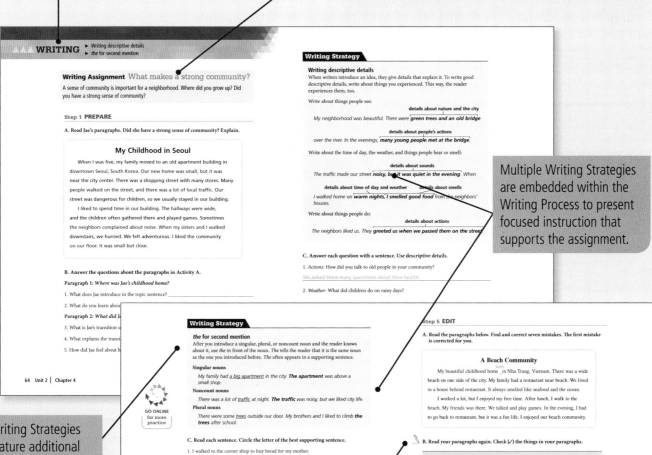

Multiple Writing Strategies are embedded within the Writing Process to present focused instruction that supports the assignment.

Writing Strategies feature additional language points and writing skills so that students become aware of paragraph organization, including main ideas and support, coherence devices, mechanics, spelling, and punctuation.

The Writing Assignment icon highlights scaffolded steps in the writing process.

Critical Thinking Questions provide further opportunities to reflect on the topic of the writing task.

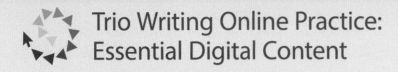

Trio Writing Online Practice: Essential Digital Content

With content that is exclusive to the digital experience, ***Trio Writing*** **Online Practice** provides multiple opportunities for skills practice and acquisition—beyond the classroom and beyond the page.

Each unit of ***Trio Writing*** is accompanied by a variety of automatically graded activities. Students' progress is recorded, tracked, and fed back to the instructor.

Grammar and Vocabulary Chants help students internalize the target grammar structure and vocabulary for greater accuracy and fluency when writing.

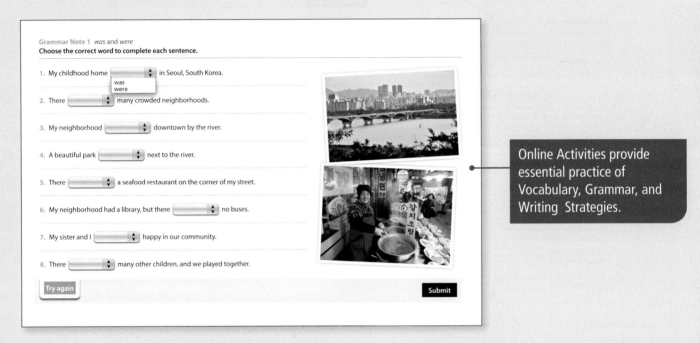

Online Activities provide essential practice of Vocabulary, Grammar, and Writing Strategies.

GO ONLINE icons lead students to essential digital content.

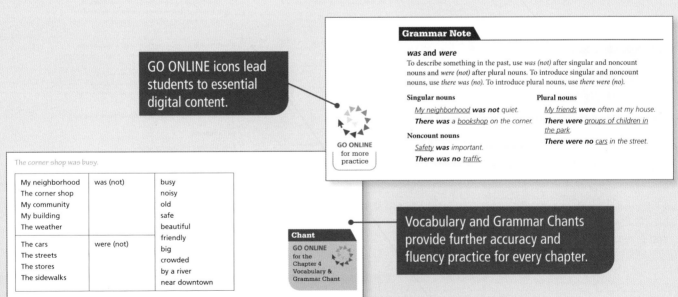

Vocabulary and Grammar Chants provide further accuracy and fluency practice for every chapter.

Use the access code on the inside front cover to log in at **www.oxfordlearn.com/login**.
Need help? Watch a tutorial video at **www.oxfordlearn.com/howtoregister**.

Readiness Unit

Words

Parts of speech
Nouns
Singular, plural, and noncount nouns
Possession with singular nouns ('s)
Verbs
    Action verbs
    Nonaction verbs
Adjectives
    Possessive adjectives

Sentences

Simple sentences
Compound sentences

Paragraphs

Writing one or two paragraphs

UNIT WRAP UP   ## Extend Your Skills

▲ WORDS

Parts of Speech

English has different parts of speech. Three parts of speech are nouns, verbs, and adjectives.

Nouns	food	music	places
Verbs	eat	play	see
Adjectives	spicy	good	new

Different words go together in English. Verbs and adjectives often go with nouns.

Verbs with nouns	eat food	play music	see places
Adjectives with nouns	spicy food	good music	new places

A. Circle two verbs that go with each noun.

1. *ride* *have* *spend* bicycles

2. *take* *visit* *see* pictures

3. *watch* *like* *complain* television

4. *eat* *spend* *save* money

5. *play* *order* *watch* soccer

6. *go* *have* *make* plans

B. Match an adjective from the box to each noun below.

crowded	careful	delicious	fast	full	tall

1. _____careful_____ shopper

2. _____ food

3. _____ streets

4. _____ mountains

5. _____ service

6. _____ price

Nouns

Nouns are people, places, and things.

People	Places	Things
a friend	*a school*	*an idea*
our family	*her neighborhood*	*many adventures*
my sister	*the country*	*a lot of information*
Mr. Lee	*a city*	*money*

Look at each noun. Is it a person, place, or thing? Check (✓) your answer.

	Person	Place	Thing
1. classmate	✓		
2. city			
3. winter			
4. product			
5. desert			
6. restaurant			
7. neighbor			
8. computer			

Singular, Plural, and Noncount Nouns

Singular means one. Use *a* or *an* before singular nouns.

    a car   *a student*   *an idea*

Plural means more than one. Add an *-s* to plural nouns.

    two rivers   *a lot of trees*   *many places*

Noncount nouns do not have a number. They do not use *a* or *an*. They do not have a plural *-s*.

    nature   *weather*   *music*

A. Look at the underlined word in each sentence. Check (✓) the correct answer.

	Singular noun	Plural noun	Noncount noun
1. She has two <u>brothers</u>.		✓	
2. My city has a <u>subway</u>.			
3. She wears <u>jewelry</u>.			
4. They are staying at a <u>hotel</u>.			
5. There is <u>information</u> for students online.			
6. I like old <u>neighborhoods</u>.			
7. Laith spends <u>money</u> on expensive electronics.			
8. There are many <u>lakes</u> in my country.			

B. Write the noun that describes each picture. Add *a* before singular nouns. Add *-s* to plural nouns.

beach	coworker	map	company	parent	tourist

1.

___parents___

2.

_____

3.

_____

4.

_____

5.

_____

6.

_____

Possession with Singular Nouns (*'s*)

Use an *apostrophe s* (*'s*) to show possession with singular nouns. The *'s* explains that a noun belongs to a person. Add *'s* to a singular noun or a name.

*My **grandmother's house** is beautiful.*

*I like my **son's smile**.*

***Samer's company** is successful.*

Use each set of words to write a complete sentence. Add *'s* to the first noun to show possession. Use a capital letter and period.

1. my / mother / smile / is / beautiful _My mother's smile is beautiful._

2. Mrs. Danelski / store / is / successful _____

3. my husband / mornings / are / busy _____

4. Alma / friend / is / a travel writer _____

5. my coworker / English / is / good _____

6. Kenji / ideas / are / interesting _____

Verbs

Action Verbs

Many verbs describe actions.

Routines	In progress now
My brother **cooks** dinner.	They **are showing** soccer on television.

Routines	In progress now
 People **meet** at work on Monday morning.	 He **is laughing**.
 Class **starts** at 9 and **finishes** at 11.	 We **are moving** to a new place.

A. Read each sentence. Fill in the blank with a verb from the box.

cooks	comes	finishes	goes	shows	wears

1. A lot of snow ____*comes*____ in winter.

2. A good shopper _____ nice clothes.

3. My grandmother _____ delicious meals for me.

4. Our teacher _____ pictures in class.

5. She _____ her class at 1 p.m.

6. My brother _____ to school in the United States.

B. Circle the verb that describes the action in each picture. Then write the sentence.

1.
The children *(are laughing)*
     are studying

The children are laughing.

2.
Mina   *is moving*
     is relaxing

_____

3.
We   *are eating*
     are studying

_____

4.
The students   *are writing*
     are talking

_____

5.
Gemini   *is swimming*
     is walking

_____

6.
They   *are traveling*
     are working

_____

Nonaction Verbs

Some verbs do not describe actions. Nonaction verbs describe people, things, and feelings.

*I **have** a busy life.*   *They **are** similar.*   *I **am** adventurous.*

*The food **smells** good.*   *He **feels** happy.*   *Mr. Lee **likes** nature.*

Circle the correct verb. Then write the sentence.

1. My grandfather   *plays*   *(is)*   intelligent.

My grandfather is intelligent.

2. A driver   *feels*   *watches*   the street.

_____

3. The man   *is*   *likes*   soccer.

_____

4. My country   *is*   *has*   nice weather.

_____

5. The chicken   *smells* *cooks*   delicious.

_____

6. My parents   *are*   *have*   similar lives.

_____

Adjectives

Adjectives describe people, places, and things.

Adjectives describe people.	Adjectives describe places.	Adjectives describe things.
*The doctor is **friendly**.* *We have a **good** teacher.*	*My city is **interesting**.* *There are **famous** stores.*	*The prices are not **cheap**.* *She buys **expensive** products.*

A. Circle two adjectives that describe each person, place, or thing.

1. (*modern*)   *happy*   (*tall*)   building
2. *fresh*   *intelligent*   *favorite*   person
3. *adventurous*   *green*   *active*   people
4. *popular*   *busy*   *red*   restaurant
5. *warm*   *hot*   *important*   weather
6. *comfortable*   *good*   *interesting*   advice

B. Write the correct adjective phrase below each picture.

a dry summer	a fun place	a loud street	wet weather
an angry crowd	serious about school	a patient mother	curious children

1.

an angry crowd

2.

3.

4.

5.

6.

7.

8.

Possessive Adjectives

Possessive adjectives show that something or someone belongs to a person. Like other adjectives, possessive adjectives come before nouns.

*I go to school. **My** class is interesting.*

*You are a student, so **your** life is busy.*

*He is tall, but **his** wife is short.*

*She lives in the United States, but **her** parents live in China.*

*We have many neighbors. **Our** neighbors are friendly.*

*They have children. **Their** children are polite.*

A. Replace the underlined words with *his* or *her*. Write the sentence.

1. My sister travels a lot. <u>My sister's</u> favorite city is Hong Kong.

   My sister travels a lot. _Her favorite city is Hong Kong._____

2. My wife likes to cook. <u>My wife's</u> food is delicious.

   My wife likes to cook. _____

3. Layla is buying a new computer. <u>Layla's</u> computer is old.

   Layla is buying a new computer. _____

4. John plays sports. <u>John's</u> favorite sport is soccer.

   John plays sports. _____

5. Mrs. Patel is intelligent. We listen to <u>Mrs. Patel's</u> advice.

   Mrs. Patel is intelligent. _____

B. Complete each sentence. Write *my, your, our,* or *their*.

1. My wife and I have two children. _____Our_____ children are curious and intelligent.

2. My coworker and her husband have five children. _____ lives are busy.

3. Customers spend _____ money carefully.

4. _____ classmate and I are different. I like cities, but she likes quiet places.

5. My friend and I like adventure. We ride _____ bicycles in the mountains.

▲▲ SENTENCES

Simple Sentences

English has different kinds of sentences. Two types of sentences are simple sentences and compound sentences. A simple sentence has one subject-verb combination.

subject + verb

Sheila visits *different cities.*

subject + verb

I am saving *money for my trip.*

A simple sentence always has one subject-verb combination, but sometimes it has two subjects or two verbs together. Use *and* to combine two subjects and two verbs.

two subjects

My brother and I *are good sons.*

two verbs

We **work** *hard* **and help** *our parents.*

A. Use the words in the chart to write simple sentences. Use a capital letter and period.

My friends and I We My classmates They	are	happy helpful funny polite responsible
	like	books clothes coffee food nature

B. Read each sentence. Circle the subject(s). Underline the verb(s).

1. The nights are cold.

2. My country has beautiful beaches. They have white sand and blue water.

3. Olga is at the store. She is buying gifts for her relatives.

4. Fish and chicken are good for you.

5. The customers and salespeople often go to a restaurant and talk about business.

6. Mr. Kovacs and his son live in the same building and work in the same bank.

Compound Sentences

A compound sentence has two subject-verb combinations. It combines two sentences with a comma and a conjunction such as *and, but,* or *so*.

Use *and* to combine sentences with similar information.

subject + verb   subject + verb

Abeba likes books, and **she reads** a lot at home.

subject + verb   subject + verb

Ikemba is active, and **we play** a lot of soccer together.

Use *but* to combine sentences that show a difference.

I like summer, but my husband likes winter.

The country is small, but it has many tourist places.

Use *so* to combine a sentence with a cause and a sentence with an effect.

Workers are busy, so they often eat in restaurants.

I want to travel, so I am saving money.

A. Circle *and* or *but*. Write the correct sentence below.

1. My sister is fashionable,   (and)   *but*   she wears nice clothes.

My sister is fashionable, and she wears nice clothes.

2. I live in London,   *and*   *but*   my favorite city is Beirut.

_____

3. I am a responsible student,   *and*   *but*   school is important to me.

_____

4. Hoang is smiling,   *and*   *but*   Tiara is angry.

_____

5. Soroya stays home,   *and*   *but*   she watches television.

_____

6. It is winter,   *and*   *but*   the weather is warm.

_____

B. Circle the letter of the phrase that best completes each sentence. Then write the correct sentence.

1. There is beautiful weather in the summer, so

   a. we often stay in the house.   (b.) we often go outside.

   There is beautiful weather in the summer, so we often go outside.

2. It is hot, so

   a. my friends and I are going to the beach.   b. my friends and I like sports.

   _____

3. We have a lot of work, so

   a. we are relaxed.   b. we are busy.

   _____

4. She is lost, so

   a. she is using a map.   b. she listens to music.

   _____

5. I walk to school, so

   a. I am a tourist.   b. I wear comfortable shoes.

   _____

6. My friend likes fashion, so

   a. she knows about computers.   b. she knows about clothes.

   _____

▲▲▲ PARAGRAPHS

Writing One or Two Paragraphs

A paragraph explains one main idea. Supporting sentences have details to explain the main idea.

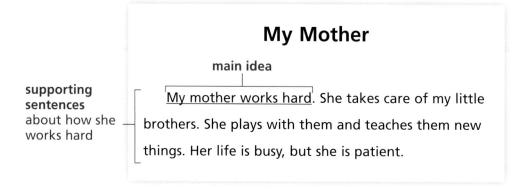

My Mother

main idea

supporting sentences about how she works hard

My mother works hard. She takes care of my little brothers. She plays with them and teaches them new things. Her life is busy, but she is patient.

Two paragraphs help writers organize information. The second paragraph often changes the focus to a different person, place, or time.

My Mother and Father

main idea

Focus 1: my mother

My parents work hard. **My mother** stays home with the children. She takes care of my little brothers. She plays with them and teaches them new things. It is a lot of work, but she is patient.

Focus 2: my father

My father is busy at work. He works at a restaurant. He starts at 8 a.m. and finishes at 5 p.m. After work, he comes home and cooks dinner for the family. He helps my mother with the house, and he reads books to my brothers at night. My parents have a long day, but they are happy.

A. Read the paragraphs. What is the writer's new focus in the second paragraph? Circle the correct answer.

1.

Costa Rica

I live in Canada. I like my country, but it snows a lot. Our winters are cold, so I want to visit a warm place.

Costa Rica has beautiful weather. Winters are warm, and there are beautiful beaches. People swim in the ocean and relax in the warm sun. I like nice weather, so it is a good place for me.

Focus of second paragraph:

a. a different person

b. a different place

c. a different time

2.

Neighbors

My neighbor Kim and I have different lives. Kim gets up at 5 a.m. She works all day, and she comes home in the afternoon. She goes to bed early.

I am different. I am a musician, so I sleep in the morning, and I get up in the afternoon. I go to cafés and play music at night. I go to bed late.

Focus of second paragraph:

a. a different person

b. a different place

c. a different time

3.

Italy

Italy has interesting cities. Rome is a famous city in Italy. Rome has many important buildings and historic neighborhoods. There are old hotels and cafés. There are green parks, and there is a big river.

Milan is a city for shoppers. Fashion is important in Milan, and there are many famous stores. They sell fashionable clothes and jewelry. Many tourists come to Milan. Prices are expensive, so they spend a lot of money.

Focus of second paragraph:

a. a different person

b. a different place

c. a different time

4.

My Food

I eat different food in summer and winter. Summer is hot, so I drink a lot of water. I eat fresh vegetables and fruit, and I do not cook a lot.

Winter is cold, so I cook hot food at home. I eat spicy seafood and chicken, and I make vegetable soup. I drink a lot of hot tea, and I stay warm.

Focus of second paragraph:

a. a different person

b. a different place

c. a different time

B. Read the statements and decide if they describe one main idea or two main ideas. Check (✓) one paragraph for one main idea or two paragraphs for two main ideas. Discuss your answer with a partner.

1. a. _____ **one paragraph**

I am not a social person. I am happy at home. I am quiet, and I read a lot of books. Sometimes I play games on my computer. My husband is social. He has a lot of friends from work. He meets them at restaurants and talks about sports. He is always on his phone.

b. __✓__ **two paragraphs**

I am not a social person. I am happy at home. I am quiet, and I read a lot of books. Sometimes I play games on my computer.

My husband is social. He has a lot of friends from work. He meets them at restaurants and talks about sports. He is always on his phone.

2. a. _____ **one paragraph**

Summer is my favorite time of the year. I visit my family in Mexico. I go to the beach with my friends and listen to the ocean. I swim in the water. I relax by the beach and read a good book. I have fun with my friends and relatives, and I feel happy.

b. _____ **two paragraphs**

Summer is my favorite time of the year. I visit my family in Mexico. I go to the beach with my friends and listen to the ocean.

I swim in the water. I relax by the beach and read a good book. I have fun with my friends and relatives, and I feel happy.

3. a. _____ **one paragraph**

I love Paris in the summer. I walk on old streets and take pictures of beautiful places. People go to cafés. They sit in the sun and drink coffee. It is beautiful. I like Casablanca in the winter. I visit my family there. We relax in my father's house and drink glasses of tea. Friends come to visit, and I feel at home.

b. _____ **two paragraphs**

I love Paris in the summer. I walk on old streets and take pictures of beautiful places. People go to cafés. They sit in the sun and drink coffee. It is beautiful.

I like Casablanca in the winter. I visit my family there. We relax in my father's house and drink glasses of tea. Friends come to visit, and I feel at home.

4. a. _____ **one paragraph**

My husband and I often cook for friends. We go to the market in the morning, and we look for fresh seafood. We also buy vegetables. We bring the food home, and we plan dinner. The food is ready in the evening. Our friends come, and they are happy.

b. _____ **two paragraphs**

My husband and I often cook for friends. We go to the market in the morning, and we look for fresh seafood.

We also buy vegetables. We bring the food home, and we plan dinner. The food is ready in the evening. Our friends come, and they are happy.

In the Readiness Unit, you reviewed words from *Trio Writing* 1 and learned new words. Look at the word bank for the Readiness Unit. Check (✓) the words you know. Circle the words you want to learn better.

OXFORD 2000 🔑

Adjectives		Nouns		Verbs
angry	late	advice	information	bring
busy	loud	brother	life	come
comfortable	modern	city	money	cook
different	patient	company	morning	feel
dry	popular	country	mother	finish
favorite	quiet	customer	neighbor	have
friendly	relaxed	father	picture	laugh
full	responsible	food	place	make
funny	serious	fun	plan	move
helpful	similar	grandfather	service	show
important	wet	grandmother	sister	smell
intelligent		house	smile	start
		husband	wife	

PRACTICE WITH THE OXFORD 2000 🔑

A. Use the words in the chart. Match adjectives with nouns.

1. comfortable place   2. _____
3. _____   4. _____
5. _____   6. _____

B. Use the words in the chart. Match verbs with nouns.

1. make plans   2. _____
3. _____   4. _____
5. _____   6. _____

C. Use the words in the chart. Match verbs with adjective noun partners.

1. have friendly neighbors   2. _____
3. _____   4. _____
5. _____   6. _____

UNIT **1** Relationships

- Use the simple present with frequency adverbs
- Use verbs with *to*
- Write paragraphs that answer different questions
- Use *when* to introduce a situation
- Write paragraphs about how you meet people

▲ VOCABULARY ▸ Oxford 2000 🔑 words to talk about meeting people

A. Write the correct number from the pictures next to each item in the box.

_____ offer to help	__1__ invite them to have lunch together	_____ introduce myself to my neighbors
_____ interrupt the meeting		
_____ close friends	_____ try to practice English	_____ compliment their house

B. Write each phrase below the correct picture.

get to know my neighbor	interrupt our meeting	live in a safe community
have a common interest in art	~~introduce myself to my new coworkers~~	share lunch

1.

introduce myself to my new coworkers

2.

_____

3.

_____

4.

_____

5.

_____

6.

_____

Oxford 2000 🔑

Use the Oxford 2000 list on page 133 to find more words to describe the pictures on these pages. Share your words with a partner.

C. Complete each sentence with a person or place. Use your own ideas.

1. I am getting to know new people at my ____school____.

2. I offer to help my _____.

3. I introduce myself to my _____.

4. I want to become closer to people in my _____.

5. I like to talk about my _____.

GO ONLINE for more practice

A. Read Marc's paragraphs. Circle the correct title.

At Work / At School

I am at a new school, so I want to make new friends. There are interesting people in my classes, and I want to get to know them. I am not a shy person. When I see my classmates in the cafeteria, I try to talk to them. Sometimes we eat lunch and practice our English together.

When we talk, I am curious, and I ask questions. I listen closely and look for common interests. I usually ask about school. We share information about our teachers. We feel closer, and we sometimes become good friends.

B. Check (✓) the picture that matches Marc's paragraphs in Activity A.

Grammar Note

The simple present with frequency adverbs

Use the simple present to talk about things that are generally true. Use the base form of a verb with *I, we, they*, and plural nouns. Use *do not* + verb to show the negative.

I **live** in a new country.	I **do not use** English at home.
When I meet new people, I **feel** happy.	We **do not interrupt** our teacher.
My classmates **study** together.	They **do not like** to talk about money.
They **have** lunch after class.	

Use the simple present and frequency adverbs like *always, usually, often, sometimes,* and *never* to show *how often* something is true. Frequency adverbs usually come before a verb.

When is it true?	Adverb	Sentence
100% of the time	*always*	I **always** *try to be friendly.*
80–90% of the time	*usually*	I **usually** *have meetings at work.*
60–70% of the time	*often*	We **often** *have lunch outside.*
10–50% of the time	*sometimes**	We **sometimes** *have lunch in the cafeteria.* **Sometimes** *we have lunch in the cafeteria.*
0% of the time	*never*	I **never** *interrupt people.*

*Sometimes can come before a subject or a verb.

GO ONLINE
for more
practice

C. Read each topic sentence below. Write supporting sentences with words from the box. Use *I/we/they + (do not) + verb*.

become closer to their neighbors	read emails from my coworkers	meet other people from the neighborhood
compliment them	practice our English	sit in the cafeteria
interrupt them	relax in the warm sun	speak other languages
write emails to friends		

1. My classmates and I usually eat outside.

   a. We do not sit in the cafeteria.

   b. We relax in the warm sun.

2. When I talk to new people, I always try to be polite.

   a. _____

   b. _____

3. When I have meetings at work, I often use my computer.

a. _____

b. _____

4. Sometimes people in the community get together.

a. _____

b. _____

5. My classmates and I always work hard in English class.

a. _____

b. _____

D. Complete each sentence with *always, often, usually, sometimes,* or *never*. There can be more than one correct answer.

1. I am polite. I _____*never*_____ interrupt people.

2. When other people compliment me, I _____ smile.

3. My coworkers _____ offer to help me.

4. My neighbors are friendly. They _____ talk a lot.

5. I _____ feel nervous when I meet new people.

6. Close friends _____ have common interests.

7. Children _____ play soccer on my street.

8. When my classmates and I have conversations, we _____ practice our English.

E. Use the words in the chart to write sentences.

I sometimes meet friends for dinner.

I	always usually often sometimes	compliment my friends forget people's names interrupt my classmates introduce myself to new people meet friends for dinner
	do not never	offer to help my neighbors practice soccer talk about sports try to be friendly

Verbs with *to*

Use *like to, offer to, try to,* and *want to* to give more information about an action, feeling, or state. Use *like to, offer to, try to,* and *want to* before a verb.

verb + *to* + verb

My friends and I **like to talk** about soccer.

verb + *to* + verb

I **offer to help** my classmates.

verb + *to* + verb

I **try to be** friendly at school.

verb + *to* + verb

We **want to know** about our community.

GO ONLINE
for more
practice

F. Unscramble the words to make sentences.

1. at home / like to / be / I   I like to be at home.

2. my friends / ask me / like to / questions   _____

3. want to / interrupt / do not / I   _____

4. help me / try to / my parents / always   _____

5. countries / I / visit / want to / other   _____

6. meet / like to / people / at school / I   _____

G. Use the words in the chart to write sentences.

My classmates like to ask questions.

I My classmates We	like to offer to try to want to	ask questions help other people make new friends meet interesting people play soccer share common interests see my family talk in English

Chant

GO ONLINE
for the
Chapter 1
Vocabulary &
Grammar Chant

Writing Assignment How do people meet?

Some people are good at meeting others. Where do you meet people? How do you get to know them?

Step 1 PREPARE

A. Read Silvia's paragraphs. What makes her family happy?

> ## In Our Neighborhood
>
> My family and I like to meet new people in our neighborhood. There are a lot of other families on our street. People sit outside and talk about their lives, and sometimes we play street games. It is a safe and friendly community.
>
> When we see new neighbors, we try to be polite. We walk over and introduce ourselves. We share information about the neighborhood and offer to help them. We want to become friends, so sometimes we invite them to our house for tea. We like to get to know our new neighbors.

Writing Strategy

Writing paragraphs that answer different questions
In the model below, the paragraphs answer different questions. The first paragraph has a topic sentence that introduces the topic. When the writer talks about the topic in a new way, a transition sentence shows the change of focus.

topic sentence

**Paragraph 1:
Where do you meet new people?**

I am at a new school, so I want to make new friends. There are interesting people in my classes, and I want to get to know them. I am not a shy person. When I see my classmates in the cafeteria, I try to talk to them. Sometimes we eat lunch and practice our English together.

transition sentence

**Paragraph 2:
How do you get to know them?**

When we talk, I am curious, and I ask questions. I listen closely and look for common interests. I usually ask about school. We share information about our teachers. We feel closer, and we sometimes become good friends.

GO ONLINE
for more
practice

B. Answer the questions about the paragraphs in Activity A.

Paragraph 1: *Where do you meet new people?*

1. What is Silvia's topic sentence? _____

2. What do people in her community do outside? _____

Paragraph 2: *How do you get to know them?*

3. What is Silvia's transition sentence? _____

4. What details show that Silvia's family is polite?

_____

_____

C. Read the paragraphs below. Choose the best transition sentence for the beginning of the second paragraph and circle it. Then write it on the line.

At Work

I work at a big company, so I meet a lot of people. My coworkers and I often have meetings. We share our ideas and solve problems together. We have common goals, so I feel comfortable around them.

_____ I compliment their good ideas. When they have a lot of work to do, I offer to help them, and I do not complain. We talk about work, but we sometimes have lunch together. We share details about our lives, and we become closer.

Transition sentence: a. When my coworkers talk, I am nervous.

b. When I make new friends, I feel happy.

c. When I work with new people, I try to stay positive.

Step 2 PREWRITE

A. Add details about the people you meet in different places and the times when you are together. Write your ideas in the chart on the next page.

Places	People I meet	When we are together
1. at school	my classmates	at lunch, after class
2. in my neighborhood		
3. at work		
4. in other countries		
5. _____ (other)		

B. **Write a topic sentence and a transition sentence. Complete one of the sentences below or write your own sentences.**

Topic sentence	Transition sentence
I often meet new people… I…, so I want to meet new people. I like to meet people at…	When I meet new people, I feel… When we talk, I… When I work with…, I try to be…

C. **Think about how you get to know others. What do you do and not do? Write your ideas in the chart below.**

I…	I do not…
say hello smile	interrupt people

Step 3 WRITE

A. **Organize your paragraphs. Use your Prewrite notes to write sentences.**

Paragraph 1: *Where do you meet new people?*

1. Where do you meet new people? Where do you see them?

2. What do they do?

_____

_____

Paragraph 2: *How do you get to know them?*

3. When you meet new people, how are you? Are you friendly, polite, or nervous?

_____

_____

4. What do you talk about or ask about?

_____

_____

5. What do you do? What do you *not* do?

_____

_____

Word Partners

share details

share (common) interests

share information

share food

share stories

_____

GO ONLINE
to practice
word partners

 B. Use your sentences from Activity A to write two paragraphs. Add a title to your paragraphs.

Step 4 REVISE

A. Read the paragraphs. Is your family similar or different?

> ### New Family, New Friends
>
> I like to meet new family members. My family is big, and my relatives live in different parts of the world. Sometimes I travel to the United States to see my brothers. When I stay with them, I get to know their new families.
>
> When my brothers introduce me, I am nervous. My new relatives are curious about my life, so they ask me a lot of questions. They want to know about our childhood in Argentina. I want to feel comfortable, so I share funny stories about my brothers. We have fun, and we become a closer family.

B. Read the paragraphs in Activity A again. Circle *when*.

when to introduce a situation

A sentence with *when* shows a relationship between two events. *When* often means "any time" or "every time." Use *when* to introduce a situation. Then explain what people do or how they feel.

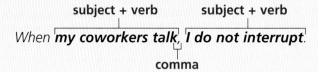

situation
|
When I see my new classmates, I try to talk to them.

situation
|
When I make new friends, I feel happy.

When joins two subject-verb combinations together. Use *when* at the beginning of a sentence. Put a comma before the second subject + verb. Put a period at the end of the sentence.

subject + verb   subject + verb
When **my coworkers talk, I do not interrupt**.
comma

GO ONLINE
for more
practice

C. Read each sentence with *when*. Underline the subject-verb combination. Then write a comma in the correct place.

1. When <u>I meet</u> new classmates, <u>I am</u> not shy.

2. When we have lunch we try to speak English.

3. When my friends get together they share new music.

4. When I take the bus I hear interesting conversations.

5. When people become friends they share details about their lives.

6. When friends are together they often watch sports.

 D. Rewrite your paragraphs from page 29. Use the questions below to help you.

Oxford 2000 🔑

Do you need more words to write about meeting people? Use the Oxford 2000 list on page 133 to find more words for your sentences.

Revising Questions

Can you:

• use *when* to introduce a situation?

• use the Oxford 2000 to add more vocabulary words?

• add details?

A. Read the paragraphs below. Find and correct seven mistakes. The first mistake is corrected for you.

Friends Around the World

comma

I meet interesting people from around the world. When I travel, I walk in city neighborhoods. I like drink coffee outside at cafés and talk to people. I make sometimes new friends.

When I want meet other people. I compliment their country. They like often to share details about the people and their history. There are difference, but we also find things in common. When I travel, I feel closer to the world.

 B. Read your paragraphs again. Check (✓) the things in your paragraphs.

Editing Checklist

○ 1. Capital letters   ○ 2. Frequency adverbs

○ 3. Periods   ○ 4. *like to/offer to/try to/want to* + verb

○ 5. *I/we/they* + verb   ○ 6. *when* to introduce a situation

 C. Now write your final paragraphs. Use the Editing Checklist to help you.

Step 6 **PUBLISH**

 Follow these steps to publish your paragraphs.

Publishing Steps

- Share your paragraphs with a partner.
- Answer the questions.
  - Which ideas do you like best in your partner's paragraphs?
  - Are you and your partner similar or different?
- Put your paragraphs in your portfolio!

Critical Thinking Question

Is it easy or difficult for you to make new friends? Why?

Who Has Good Social Skills?

- Use the simple present with *he* and *she*
- Use frequency adverbs with *be*
- Write a concluding sentence

- Use *it* with *when* to explain a feeling
- Write paragraphs describing a host with good social skills

▲ VOCABULARY ▶ Oxford 2000 🔑 words to describe social skills

A. Write the correct number from the pictures next to each item in the box.

_____ take off our shoes		_____ the center of the family		_____ a place to relax outside	
_____ greet people at the door		1 accept an invitation		_____ an apartment full of relatives	

B. Circle the correct phrase to describe each picture.

1.

   (enjoy our evening)

   enjoy our guests

2.

   feel welcome

   feel ignored

3.

   bring news

   bring food

4.

   a neighborhood full of houses

   a neighborhood full of apartments

5.

   a place to enjoy guests

   a place to relax

6.

   a polite host

   an impolite host

Oxford 2000 🔑

Use the Oxford 2000 list on page 133 to find more words to describe the pictures on these pages. Share your words with a partner.

C. Write the phrases in the correct boxes to describe what hosts and guests do. Share your answers with a partner.

accept invitations	bring gifts	take off their shoes at the door
c̶o̶o̶k̶ f̶o̶o̶d̶	make guests feel welcome	greet people at the door
invite people for dinner	s̶a̶y̶ t̶h̶a̶n̶k̶ y̶o̶u̶	

Hosts...	Guests...
cook food	say thank you

GO ONLINE
for more practice

A. Read the paragraphs. Why is the grandmother important?

The Center of the Family

My grandmother is the center of our family. People visit her all day, and her apartment is always full of relatives. They come and bring food, and there are interesting conversations.

My grandmother greets us at the door when we come. We take off our shoes and go into the living room. My grandmother asks about changes in our lives, and we tell her about school and family. Sometimes her neighbors stop by and bring news about the community. It is fun when we are together. My grandmother's house is always a comfortable place to relax with family and friends.

B. Read the sentences about the paragraphs in Activity A. Check (✓) the sentences that are true.

_____ 1. Her apartment is a quiet place.

_____ 2. Guests wear their shoes in the living room.

_____ 3. Neighbors like to visit.

_____ 4. There are different conversations.

_____ 5. Friends and family come together.

Grammar Note

The simple present with *he* and *she*

Use the simple present with *he* and *she* to talk about what someone likes, has, or does frequently. Use the simple present with *it* to describe a thing or situation. Add an *-s* to a verb with *he, she,* and *it*.

  *My grandmother **greets** us at the door, and she **says** hello.*

  *My friend Oliver **likes** to travel. He **talks** about his trips to different countries.*

  *The living room **smells** good. It **has** fresh flowers.*

Sometimes the simple present has a different spelling with *he, she,* and *it*. Note the different spelling rules on the next page.

Spelling rules	Examples
Add -es to a verb that ends in -s, -x, -z, -ch, or -sh	*My grandfather **relaxes** outside.* *He **dresses** for the warm weather.* *My grandmother **watches** the food.* *She **finishes** dinner.*
Add -ies to a verb that ends in a consonant + *y*.	*My friend **studies** social skills at college.* *She **tries** to understand people.*
Use *goes* and *has*.	*He **goes** to other countries.* *She **has** many interesting stories.*

Use *does not* + verb to show the negative with *he*, *she*, and *it* in the simple present.

*My friend is polite, and she **does not interrupt** people.*
*It is usually hot outside, but he **does not complain**.*
*Her house is in a historic neighborhood, but it **does not look** old.*

GO ONLINE
for more
practice

C. Read the topic sentence. Then write supporting sentences about Mercy. Explain what she does and does not do. Use ideas from the box.

Topic sentence: Mercy is a polite guest.

ask polite questions	compliment people's homes	try to be helpful
bring all her friends	interrupt conversations	ignore other guests

1. She asks polite questions. _____

2. _____

3. _____

4. _____

5. _____

6. _____

D. Read the sentences. Fill in each blank with the correct form of a verb from the box.

feel	make	tell

1. My father has good social skills. He _____*feels*_____ comfortable around people. He is funny. When he ____*tells*____ stories, he ____*makes*____ people laugh.

ask	go	talk

2. Mrs. Gutierrez is a social person. When she _____ outside, she _____ to her neighbors. Sometimes she _____ them for advice.

have	live	play

3. Sometimes I visit my friend in New York. He _____ in a small apartment. He _____ noisy neighbors, so he usually _____ loud music.

greet	offer	invite

4. My sister enjoys time with friends, and she often _____ them to her house after work. She _____ them at the door, and she _____ them something to drink.

enjoy	go	relax

5. My grandmother is a quiet person. When the weather is good, she _____ outside and _____. She drinks hot coffee and _____ nature.

invite	read	try

6. My friend Megan sometimes _____ me for dinner. She _____ books about food. She _____ to use new ideas in her cooking, so her meals are always interesting.

E. Use the words in the chart to write sentences.

A good host has interesting ideas to share.

| A fun host
A popular host
A good host
He
She | has | interesting ideas to share
many guests
intelligent conversations with others
good social skills |
| | is | a good person to know
always at the center of the conversation
comfortable around people
friendly to others |

Grammar Note

Frequency adverbs with *be*

In Chapter 1, you learned about frequency adverbs (*always, usually, often, sometimes, never*). Frequency adverbs usually come after the verb *be* (*am, is, are*).

> I **am** always busy at school.

> Her apartment **is** usually full of relatives.

> Our conversations **are** never boring.

Use *sometimes* after the verb *be* or at the beginning of a sentence.

> She is **sometimes** outside.

> **Sometimes** she is outside.

GO ONLINE
for more
practice

F. Rewrite each sentence. Add a frequency adverb from the box to describe your life. The adverbs can be used more than once.

always	usually	often	sometimes	never

1. I am polite. *I am always polite.* _____

2. My mother is a good host. _____

3. My house is full of people. _____

4. In my city, the weather is beautiful. _____

5. It is warm in the evenings. _____

6. My friends and I are outside. _____

Chant

GO ONLINE
for the
Chapter 2
Vocabulary &
Grammar Chant

▲▲▲ WRITING
▶ Writing a concluding sentence
▶ *it* with *when* to explain a feeling

Writing Assignment Who has good social skills?

Good hosts have important social skills. Who is a good host you know? What does he or she do?

Step 1 PREPARE

A. Read the paragraphs. Is Oliver an interesting person?

A Good Host

Our neighbor Oliver has good social skills. Oliver is from England, but he and his wife live in the United States. When the weather is nice, they often invite guests for English tea. They are good hosts, so I always accept their invitation.

When we come to the door, Oliver and his wife greet us with friendly smiles. We sit outside together, and they offer us hot tea and small sandwiches. Oliver travels a lot for work, so he often talks about his adventures in other countries. It is fun when he tells stories. When we visit Oliver, we learn details about the world from our own little neighborhood.

B. Answer the questions about the paragraphs in Activity A.

Paragraph 1: *Who is a good host?*

1. What is the topic sentence? _____

2. Where is Oliver from? _____

3. Where does he live? _____

4. When does he have guests? _____

Paragraph 2: *What does he do?*

5. What is the transition sentence? _____

6. What details show that Oliver is a good host? _____

7. What does the writer learn? Why? _____

Writing a concluding sentence

Paragraphs usually begin with a topic sentence or a transition sentence. At the end of the last paragraph, writers often include a concluding sentence.

A concluding sentence finishes all of your ideas. It often has a statement about what a writer learns or understands from an experience. It does not include new details.

topic sentence

My grandmother is the center of our family. People visit her all day, and her apartment is always full of relatives. They come and bring food, and there are interesting conversations.

transition sentence

My grandmother greets us at the door when we come. We take off our shoes and go into the living room. My grandmother asks about changes in our lives, and we talk about our plans. Sometimes neighbors come and bring news about the community. It is fun when we are together. **My grandmother's house is always a comfortable place to relax with family and friends.**

concluding sentence

GO ONLINE
for more practice

C. Read the paragraphs below. Choose the best concluding sentence and circle it. Then write it on the line.

In Paris with Liliane

When I visit my friend Liliane in Paris, I always feel welcome. Liliane is an old friend from school. She has a family and works hard. She is busy, but she does not ignore her friends. She enjoys time with them.

Liliane is a great host. When I go to Paris, she invites me for lunch. She always asks questions about my trip. She gives me good advice about restaurants and hotels. We share a common interest in art, so she takes me to museums. It is fun when we walk together. Sometimes she gets lost, and we laugh. _____

Concluding sentence: a. Liliane has children, and her husband is a nice person.

b. I always learn about places in Paris when I visit Liliane.

c. I like to go shopping in Paris, but the prices are expensive.

A. Think about a person who is a good host. Use the organizer to develop your ideas. Write the person's name at the top. Then add details about *who, when,* and *where.*

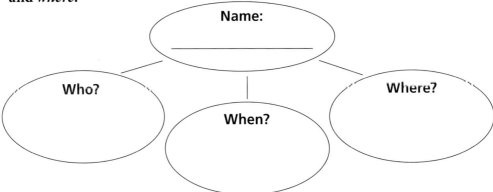

B. Write a topic sentence and a transition sentence. Complete one of the sentences below or write your own sentences.

Topic sentence	Transition sentence
… is a good host. … has good social skills, and he/she enjoys guests. When I visit…, I always have fun.	When we come to the door,… … greets us with a friendly smile. … always makes his/her guests feel welcome.

C. Think about your time with the person you are describing. How is he or she a good host? What do you do together? Write your ideas in the chart.

He/She…	I/We…
asks questions	have good conversations

D. Write your concluding sentence. Complete one of the sentences below or write your own sentence.

Concluding sentence
His/her house is a good place to… When I visit…, I learn about… I feel… when I visit…

A. Organize your paragraphs. Use your Prewrite notes to write sentences.

Paragraph 1: *Who is a good host?*

1. What is your topic sentence? _____

2. What details from Prewrite do you want to include?

_____

_____

Paragraph 2: *What does he or she do?*

3. What is your transition sentence? _____

4. What details from Prewrite do you want to include?

_____

_____

5. What is your concluding sentence? _____

B. Use your sentences from Activity A to write two paragraphs. Add a title to your paragraphs.

Word Partners

bring family

bring food

bring friends

bring gifts

bring news

GO ONLINE
to practice
word partners

A. Read the paragraphs. What kind of person is Sheida?

Dinner with My Sister

My sister Sheida likes to invite guests to her home for dinner. She has a modern apartment and a big dining room. It has a beautiful view of the city, and it is my favorite place to eat. We always enjoy our evening when we visit.

Sheida makes her guests feel comfortable. She greets us at the door, and she offers us something to drink. When we go to the dining room, there are beautiful flowers on the table. It is nice when the family sits together. We enjoy good food and conversation. Sheida's home is a good place to eat and be happy.

B. Read the paragraphs in Activity A again. Circle *when*.

it with *when* to explain a feeling

Use *it* + *be* + adjective with *when* to explain how you feel about a situation.

It is interesting when *new guests arrive.*

It is nice when *the family sits together.*

It is funny when *Oliver tells stories.*

When you use *when* at the beginning of a sentence, use a comma before the second subject-verb combination. Do not use a comma when you use *when* in the middle of a sentence.

comma

When we are together, *it is fun.*

no comma

It is relaxing **when we stay home**.

GO ONLINE
for more
practice

C. Write the letter of the phrase on the right to complete each sentence on the left. Then write the correct sentence below. Use a comma when necessary.

1. __d__ My grandmother is happy   a. when summer comes.

2. _____ We enjoy good food   b. our house is full of people.

3. _____ When the weather is nice   c. when I travel.

4. _____ I learn about different places   d. when she has guests.

5. _____ When we invite our family to eat e. when my sister cooks dinner.

6. _____ It is warm outside   f. I sit outside.

1. My grandmother is happy when she has guests.

2. _____

3. _____

4. _____

5. _____

6. _____

 D. Rewrite your paragraphs from page 41. Use the questions below to help you.

Revising Questions

Can you:

- use *it* with *when*? (e.g., *It is nice/funny when...*)

- use the Oxford 2000 to add more vocabulary words?

- add details?

A. Read the paragraphs below. Find and correct eight mistakes. The first mistake is corrected for you.

The Center of Our Neighborhood

My friend Brita likes children, and her house is the center of our

neighborhood. She ~~haves~~ has five children, and her house always is busy. Boys

and girls in the neighborhood are often there, their parents stay and talk.

Brita does not greets her guests at the door. When I come the door

is usually open. I walk into the living room and sit with other parents.

We always talk about our children. The children usually are outside.

They are happy, when the weather is nice. It always interesting when I

visit Brita's house.

B. Read your paragraphs again. Check (✓) the things in your paragraphs.

Editing Checklist

○ 1. Capital letters   ○ 2. *does not* + verb

○ 3. Periods   ○ 4. Frequency adverbs after *be*

○ 5. *-s*, *-es*, or *-ies* on verbs with *he/she*   ○ 6. *it* with *when* to explain a feeling

C. Now write your final paragraphs. Use the Editing Checklist to help you.

Step 6 PUBLISH

Follow these steps to publish your paragraphs.

Publishing Steps

• Share your paragraphs with a partner.

• Answer the questions.

  • Which ideas do you like best in your partner's paragraphs?

  • What do you learn from the paragraphs?

• Put your paragraphs in your portfolio!

Critical Thinking Question

What social skills are important for guests to have?

CHAPTER 3

How Do Places Change Us?

- Use gerunds as subjects
- Use *have/has to* + verb
- Write paragraphs about different places

- Use *because* to explain why
- Write paragraphs explaining how places change your behavior

▲ **VOCABULARY** ▶ Oxford 2000 🔑 words to talk about how people behave in different places

A. Write the correct number from the pictures next to each item in the box.

_____ pay attention to my teacher	_____ bargain with salespeople	_____ rude behavior
__1__ wait for my turn	_____ search for things on sale	_____ not respecting the rules
_____ dress inappropriately	_____ shouting in the library	

B. Write each phrase below the correct picture.

stand in line	pay attention to our teacher	act appropriately in the library
rude behavior	understand the classroom rules	~~respect our culture~~

1.

respect our culture

2.

_____

3.

_____

4.
Be on time.
Be prepared.
Be respectful.
_____

Oxford 2000 🔑

Use the Oxford 2000 list on page 133 to find more words to describe the pictures on these pages. Share your words with a partner.

5.

_____

6.
_____

C. Check (✓) the places where you do each action. Some items can have more than one check. Share your answers with a partner.

	In class	At home	With my friends
1. pay attention to behavior			
2. respect the rules			
3. dress appropriately			
4. wait for my turn			

GO ONLINE for more practice

▲▲ GRAMMAR
► Gerunds as subjects
► *have/has to* + verb

A. Read the paragraphs. Where is the writer from?

In Two Cultures

My behavior changes when I shop in different countries. In Vietnam, I bargain with salespeople because I want to save money. Sometimes other customers interrupt our conversations. We do not mind because it is our culture and interrupting other people is not bad.

In the United States, I have to change my behavior. Salespeople do not change prices, so I do not bargain. Getting a good deal is important to me, so I have to find things on sale. I stand in line quietly, and I have to wait for my turn. I am respectful because I understand American culture.

B. Check (✓) the picture that matches the paragraphs in Activity A.

Gerunds as subjects

A gerund is a noun. Writers often use a gerund or gerund phrase as the subject of a sentence. To make a gerund, add -*ing* to a verb.

gerund

Bargaining *saves me money.*

gerund phrase

Shouting in the library *is not respectful.*

A gerund subject always takes a singular verb.

Being polite **is** *important.*
Visiting my family **makes** *me happy.*

GO ONLINE
for more practice

C. Read each sentence. Underline the gerund phrase. Circle the verb.

1. Being with my family brings me happiness.

2. Having good social skills is important.

3. Listening to music relaxes me.

4. Living closer to my sister makes me feel happy.

5. Welcoming new neighbors is important in my culture.

6. Dressing appropriately for work shows respect.

7. Ignoring people is disrespectful.

8. Being in a safe community is important to my family.

D. Use the words in the chart to write sentences.

Working hard makes me proud.

Being outside	makes me	angry
Meeting new people	makes people	curious
Learning about other cultures		excited
Getting a bargain		happy
Seeing rude behavior		nervous
Working hard		proud
Having children		relaxed
		tired

E. Use a gerund subject to write your own sentence about each idea below.

1. make new friendships *Making new friendships takes time.*

2. practice English at home _____ _____

3. respect my teacher's rules _____

4. be a good student _____

5. argue with salespeople _____

6. enjoy time with my friends _____

Grammar Note

have/has to + verb

Use *have/has to* + verb to show that something is necessary or important to do.

> *In class, I **have to speak** English.*
>
> *When we visit our neighbors, we **have to be** respectful.*
>
> *Sometimes my teacher **has to ask** noisy students to be quiet.*

Use *do/does not* + *have to* + verb to show that something is not necessary.

> *At home, I **do not have to be** quiet.*
>
> *In my country, people **do not have to pay** for school.*
>
> *My grandfather **does not have to work**.*

GO ONLINE
for more
practice

F. Circle the letter of the phrase that best completes each sentence. Then write the correct sentence.

1. I am learning English, so

   a. I have to practice every day.

   b. I do not have to practice every day.

   I am learning English, so I have to practice every day.

2. I want to save money, so

   a. I have to search for bargains.

   b. I do not have to search for bargains.

   _____

3. I am living in a new country, so

    a. I have to understand the culture.

    b. I do not have to understand the culture.

_____

4. My friends understand me, so

    a. I have to change my behavior.

    b. I do not have to change my behavior.

_____

5. The room is quiet, so

    a. we have to shout.

    b. we do not have to shout.

_____

6. She is going to work, so

    a. she has to dress appropriately.

    b. she does not have to dress appropriately.

_____

G. Use the words in the chart to write sentences.

At work, I have to be polite.

| At work,
At school,
In class,
At home,
In my country, | I
we
people | have to | be polite
be respectful
be serious
dress appropriately
help other people |
| | | do not have to | pay attention to details
respect other people
study a lot
work hard |

Chant

GO ONLINE for the Chapter 3 Vocabulary & Grammar Chant

Writing Assignment How do places change us?

Places often change the way people behave. What places change your behavior? How do you act differently from one place to another place?

Step 1 PREPARE

A. Read Whitney's paragraphs. Where do her children act differently?

Inside and Outside

Being in nature changes my children's behavior. At home, they are often on their phones and computers. My daughter texts her friends, and my son sits at his computer. Sometimes we try to play a game together, but they argue, so I take them outside for a bike ride.

In nature, my children are active and curious. We often ride our bicycles to a lake near our house. They play together in the water, and they do not argue. They become different people. They are happy because they forget about their phones and computers.

B. Answer the questions about the paragraphs in Activity A.

Paragraph 1: *place 1*

1. What do Whitney's children often do at home? _____

2. When does she take her children outside? _____

Paragraph 2: *place 2*

3. How do Whitney's children feel in nature? _____

4. What details show that the children are active? _____

5. How do the children change? _____

Writing paragraphs about different places

Write two paragraphs to describe different places. Begin with a topic sentence to introduce the difference. Then use prepositional phrases to introduce each place such as *at home, at school, at work, in class, in my country,* or *in nature.* Begin a new paragraph for the second place.

topic sentence

Being in nature changes my children's behavior. At home, they are often on their phones. *My daughter texts her friends, and my son...*

In nature, my children are active and curious. We often ride our bicycles to a lake near our house. They play together in the water, and they...

GO ONLINE
for more practice

C. Read the paragraphs below. Choose the correct sentence from the box for each paragraph. Write it on the line.

In the school cafeteria, I am with my friends.   In class, I behave differently.

At School

My behavior changes when I am in school. _____

_____ We tell funny stories while we eat, and we laugh a lot. We are loud, but we are not rude. Being together makes us feel comfortable.

_____ I am serious, and I pay attention to my teacher. Sometimes other classmates are disrespectful. During class, they talk and text, and they do not pay attention. I am different because respecting teachers is important to me.

Step 2 PREWRITE

A. Write places that make you experience the different feelings below. Then choose two of the places for your paragraphs.

Feeling	comfortable	nervous	happy	serious	relaxed
Place	home				

B. Write a topic sentence. Complete one of the sentences below or write your own sentence.

Topic sentence
Being in/at...   ... changes my behavior. I behave differently when...

C. What do you do in each place? Write your two places in the chart below. Then add ideas about each place.

	What do you do? What do you not do?	What do you have to do? What do you not have to do?
Place 1: _____		
Place 2: _____		

Step 3 WRITE

A. Organize your paragraphs. Use your Prewrite notes to write sentences.

Paragraph 1: *place 1*

1. What is your topic sentence? _____

2. What is the first place, and what do you do there? _____

3. What details from Prewrite do you want to include?

_____

_____

Paragraph 2: *place 2*

4. What is the second place, and what do you do there? _____

5. What details from Prewrite do you want to include?

_____

_____

Word Partners

behave differently

do (something) differently

dress differently

talk differently

think differently

GO ONLINE
to practice
word partners

B. Use your sentences from Activity A to write two paragraphs. Add a title to your paragraphs.

Step 4 REVISE

A. Read the paragraphs. Why is the writer different?

With My Sister and My Brother

I am different when I visit my sister and brother. With my sister, I have to watch my children. We try to have a conversation, but our children always want to run around the house, and they make a lot of noise. They often interrupt us, but we do not mind because raising our children together makes us happy.

With my brother, I talk differently because he does not have children. He is young, and he is going to school. He reads many books, and we have serious conversations. Visiting my brother is interesting because I learn new ideas. I do not talk about my children because our lives are different.

B. Read the paragraphs in Activity A again. Circle *because*.

Writing Strategy

because to explain why
Use *because* to show why something happens or why something is true. *Because* combines two subject-verb combinations into one sentence.

Why do I bargain?

I bargain **because I want to save money**.

Why are they happy?

My children are happy outside **because they forget about their phones**.

Why is it important?

Being polite is important **because it shows respect**.

GO ONLINE
for more
practice

C. Circle the letter of the phrase that best completes each sentence. Then write the correct sentence.

1. I listen to my grandmother because

    a. she asks me questions.   b. I respect her.

I listen to my grandmother because I respect her.

2. Being at home makes me feel relaxed because

    a. I am with my family.   b. I am polite.

3. I respect my teacher because

    a. she texts in class.   b. she works hard.

4. People in my country have to be polite because

    a. they do not like to smile.   b. it is important in our culture.

5. In class, I am quiet because

    a. I have to pay attention.   b. I talk to my classmates.

 D. Rewrite your paragraphs from page 53. Use the questions below to help you.

Revising Questions

Can you:

- use *because* to explain a reason?
- add a concluding sentence with *because*? (e.g., *I am different because...*)
- use the Oxford 2000 to add more vocabulary words?
- add details?

Step 5 EDIT

A. Read the paragraphs below. Find and correct eight mistakes. The first mistake is corrected for you.

Mario and Me

My friend Mario and I are serious but fun. At work, we _are_ responsible. Mario and I work at a restaurant, and we have be respectful. We dress appropriately. We are polite, we pay attention to details. We work hard. Because we respect our customers.

When Mario and I are not at work. We act differently. On weekends, we are adventurous. We like to go to the mountains. Enjoying nature make us forget about work. Mario and I friends because understand each other.

B. Read your paragraphs again. Check (✓) the things in your paragraphs.

Editing Checklist

- ○ 1. Capital letters
- ○ 2. _have/has to_ + verb
- ○ 3. Periods
- ○ 4. _do/does not have to_ + verb
- ○ 5. Gerunds as subjects
- ○ 6. _because_ to explain why

C. Now write your final paragraphs. Use the Editing Checklist to help you.

Step 6 PUBLISH

Follow these steps to publish your paragraphs.

Publishing Steps

- Share your paragraphs with a partner.
- Answer the questions.
  - Which ideas do you find interesting in your partner's paragraphs?
  - Do you and your partner behave differently? How?
- Put your paragraphs in your portfolio!

Critical Thinking Question

What places do you visit to change how you feel? Why?

Look at the word bank for Unit 1. Check (✓) the words you know. Circle the words you want to learn better.

OXFORD 2000 🔑

Adjectives	Nouns		Verbs	
close	apartment	interest	accept	offer
common	attention	invitation	act	pay
other	behavior	library	become	practice
polite	center	line	dress	respect
rude	community	meeting	enjoy	search
safe	culture	news	get (to)	share
social	detail	rule	help	shout
	door	sale	ignore	stand
	evening	skill	interrupt	take (off)
	guest	turn	introduce	talk (about)
			invite	try (to)
			look (for)	understand
			(not) mind	

PRACTICE WITH THE OXFORD 2000 🔑

A. Use the words in the chart. Match adjectives with nouns.

1. _safe community_ 2. _____

3. _____ 4. _____

5. _____ 6. _____

B. Use the words in the chart. Match verbs with nouns.

1. _understand rules_ 2. _____

3. _____ 4. _____

5. _____ 6. _____

C. Use the words in the chart. Match verbs with adjective noun partners.

1. _practice polite behavior_ 2. _____

3. _____ 4. _____

5. _____ 6. _____

UNIT **2** Cities

CHAPTER **4**

What Makes a Strong Community?

▲ **VOCABULARY** — Oxford 2000 ⚷ words to talk about your childhood community

▲▲ **GRAMMAR** — The simple past tense with *-ed* and *had* *was* and *were*

▲▲▲ **WRITING** — Writing descriptive details *the* for second mention

CHAPTER **5**

What Did Your City Build?

▲ **VOCABULARY** — Oxford 2000 ⚷ words to talk about cities

▲▲ **GRAMMAR** — Irregular past tense verbs Negative past tense with *did not*

▲▲▲ **WRITING** — Using time expressions Comparative adjectives

CHAPTER **6**

How Did a Place Surprise You?

▲ **VOCABULARY** — Oxford 2000 ⚷ words to tell stories about experiences

▲▲ **GRAMMAR** — The past progressive Adjective + infinitive

▲▲▲ **WRITING** — Putting background information before the topic sentence Verbs with *that* in a conclusion

UNIT WRAP UP — ## Extend Your Skills

What Makes a Strong Community?

- Use the simple past with *-ed* and *had*
- Use *was* and *were*
- Write descriptive details

- Use *the* for second mention
- Write paragraphs about your childhood community

▲ VOCABULARY ► Oxford 2000 ✎ words to talk about your childhood community

A. Write the correct number from the pictures next to each item in the box.

_____ at a shop on the corner	_____ a strong community	_____ meeting in the local park
_____ downstairs neighbors	_____ a healthy life	_1_ lived downtown
_____ joined a noisy group	_____ a wide sidewalk	_____ a bridge across the river

B. Write each phrase below the correct picture.

a happy childhood	~~gathered on the bridge in the evening~~	a strong friendship
hurried across the busy street	visited friends downtown	meeting at a local store

1.

gathered on the bridge in the evening

2.

_____

3.

_____

4.

_____

5.

_____

6.

_____

Oxford 2000 🔑

Use the Oxford 2000 list on page 133 to find more words to describe the pictures on these pages. Share your words with a partner.

C. Circle two words that pair with the first word.

1. safe	*neighborhood*	*streets*	*bread*
2. strong	*community*	*traffic*	*family*
3. noisy	*friends*	*games*	*bench*
4. healthy	*people*	*fountain*	*dinner*
5. wide	*neighbor*	*river*	*sidewalk*
6. local	*shops*	*park*	*city*

GO ONLINE for more practice

A. Read the paragraphs. Did you live in a similar or different neighborhood as a child?

Uskudar

I had a wonderful childhood in Istanbul, Turkey. I lived in Uskudar. It was a historic neighborhood with small streets and wide sidewalks. There were old trees and parks, so it was a healthy place for children. There was a shop on the corner, so I smelled fresh bread and flowers when I walked to school.

My friends and I played together. On nice days, we gathered outside. We greeted our neighbors. Old people sat on benches and told stories. Women walked to the shops because they liked to meet each other. Men stood on the sidewalk and talked about the local news. I liked my neighborhood because we had a strong community, and I had many good times with friends.

B. What made the writer's community strong? Check (✓) the details from the paragraphs in Activity A.

_____ 1. nature and trees

_____ 2. friendly neighbors

_____ 3. a combination of old people and young people

_____ 4. traffic

_____ 5. history

_____ 6. shops in the neighborhood

Grammar Note

The simple past tense with *-ed* and *had*
Use the simple past tense to describe things that happened or were true in the past.

*In the past, we **played** games.*
*When I was a child, I **walked** to school every morning.*
*Last summer, she **visited** our home.*

Add -*ed* to regular verbs	Add -*d* to words that end in -*e*	Other -*ed* verbs change spelling
help + ed = helped	*live + d = lived*	*hurry = hurried*
play + ed = played	*move + d = moved*	*try = tried*
walk + ed = walked	*ignore + d = ignored*	*shop = shopped*

Use *had* for the simple past of both *has* and *have*.

> I **had** a wonderful childhood.
> He **had** a nice apartment.

GO ONLINE
for more practice

C. Read the paragraph. Underline the verbs. Then rewrite the paragraph. Change all the verbs to the simple past tense.

I <u>live</u> in a busy neighborhood, but I <u>like</u> it. I enjoy city life. I greet my friends. We gather on street corners and share local news. We walk together and hurry across busy streets. We shop and talk about the weather. Sometimes we walk to a local park and join other children from the neighborhood.

I lived in a busy neighborhood, but I liked it.

_____

_____

_____

_____

D. Use the words in the chart to write sentences.

I played games on our street.

I	hurried to school	on our street
My friends and I	joined a group of neighbors	in the evening
My relatives	lived in a small house	on the bridge
The neighbors	played games	in the morning
My parents	walked to local shops	
My brothers and sisters	shopped at the corner store	
	had a healthy life	

E. Complete the simple past sentences with your own ideas.

1. When guests arrived, I served _tea._ _____

2. My group of friends liked _____

3. My family enjoyed _____

4. My neighbors respected _____

5. Our neighborhood had _____

6. Old people gathered _____

Grammar Note

was and *were*

To describe something in the past, use *was (not)* after singular and noncount nouns and *were (not)* after plural nouns. To introduce singular and noncount nouns, use *there was (no)*. To introduce plural nouns, use *there were (no)*.

Singular nouns

My neighborhood **was not** quiet.

There was a <u>bookshop</u> on the corner.

Noncount nouns

Safety **was** important.

There was no <u>traffic</u>.

Plural nouns

My friends **were** often at my house.

There were <u>groups of children in the park</u>.

There were no <u>cars</u> in the street.

GO ONLINE
for more
practice

F. Complete each sentence with *there was (no)* or *there were (no)*.

1. The bridge was closed to traffic. _____ _There were no_ _____ cars.

2. We lived downtown. _____ many people on the sidewalks.

3. Our neighborhood was green in the summer because _____ a lot of rain.

4. We liked our community. _____ nice neighbors, and they helped each other.

5. Our neighborhood had a small park, so _____ a place to play.

6. Our street was quiet at night. _____ noise.

G. Use the words in each box to describe the photo. Use *there was* or *there were*. You do not need to use all the words.

1.

traffic	fresh air	fountain
trees	snow	
bench	group of people	

a. There was no traffic. _____

b. _____

c. _____

d. _____

2.

cars	sidewalks	buildings
river	shoppers	noise
forest	park	

a. There were cars. _____

b. _____

c. _____

d. _____

H. Write sentences about your childhood home. Use the words in the chart or your own ideas.

The corner shop was busy.

My neighborhood The corner shop My community My building The weather	was (not)	busy noisy old safe beautiful friendly big crowded by a river near downtown
The cars The streets The stores The sidewalks	were (not)	

Chant

GO ONLINE
for the
Chapter 4
Vocabulary &
Grammar Chant

Writing Assignment What makes a strong community?

A sense of community is important for a neighborhood. Where did you grow up? Did you have a strong sense of community?

Step 1 PREPARE

A. Read Jae's paragraphs. Did she have a strong sense of community? Explain.

My Childhood in Seoul

When I was five, my family moved to an old apartment building in downtown Seoul, South Korea. Our new home was small, but it was near the city center. There was a shopping street with many stores. Many people walked on the street, and there was a lot of local traffic. Our street was dangerous for children, so we usually stayed in our building.

I liked to spend time in our building. The hallways were wide, and the children often gathered there and played games. Sometimes the neighbors complained about noise. When my sisters and I walked downstairs, we hurried. We felt adventurous. I liked the community on our floor. It was small but close.

B. Answer the questions about the paragraphs in Activity A.

Paragraph 1: *Where was Jae's childhood home?*

1. What does Jae introduce in the topic sentence? _____

2. What do you learn about her community? _____

Paragraph 2: *What did Jae or other people do there?*

3. What is Jae's transition sentence? _____

4. What explains the transition sentence? _____

5. How did Jae feel about her childhood community? _____

Writing descriptive details

When writers introduce an idea, they give details that explain it. To write good descriptive details, write about things you experienced. This way, the reader experiences them, too.

Write about things people see:

details about nature and the city

My neighborhood was beautiful. There were **green trees and an old bridge**

details about people's actions

over the river. In the evenings, **many young people met at the bridge***.*

Write about the time of day, the weather, and things people hear or smell:

details about sounds

The traffic made our street **noisy, but it was quiet in the evening***. When*

details about time of day and weather   details about smells

I walked home on **warm nights, I smelled good food** *from the neighbors'*
houses.

Write about things people do:

details about actions

The neighbors liked us. They **greeted us when we passed them on the street***.*

GO ONLINE
for more
practice

C. Answer each question with a sentence. Use descriptive details.

1. *Actions:* How did you talk to old people in your community?

We asked them many questions about their health.

2. *Weather:* What did children do on rainy days?

_____

3. *Things people see:* What did the buildings look like in your neighborhood?

_____

4. *Smell:* What did you smell in the shops or street?

_____

A. Draw a picture of your childhood neighborhood. Then discuss your picture with a partner. Ask and answer these questions.

1. Where did you live?

2. What was interesting in your neighborhood?

3. Where did you walk?

4. What was important about your community?

5. Who did you visit?

B. Write a topic sentence and a transition sentence. Complete one of the sentences below or write your own sentences.

Topic sentence	Transition sentence
I had a beautiful/friendly/ interesting childhood in… My childhood in… was… My childhood was special because I lived in…	I had many… experiences in… I had a(n)… life there. My life there was…

C. Write your sentences in the chart below. Then write notes for your detail sentences.

Topic sentence:	Transition sentence:
Notes:	Notes:

Step 3 WRITE

A. Organize your paragraphs. Use your Prewrite notes to write sentences.

Paragraph 1: *Where was your childhood home?*

1. What is your topic sentence? _____

2. What details from Prewrite do you want to include about the community?

_____

_____

Paragraph 2: *What did you do there?*

3. What is your transition sentence? _____

4. What did you and other people do?

_____

_____

B. Use your sentences from Activity A to write two paragraphs. Add a title to your paragraphs.

Step 4 REVISE

A. Read the paragraphs below. What makes this writer's childhood home a strong community?

My Childhood Home

My childhood home was in the mountains in Mexico. I lived in Taxco. There were colorful houses in our neighborhood, and many neighbors had flowers. The streets were safe, and there was a park in the city center. The park had trees, benches, and a fountain.

I enjoyed my childhood in Taxco. My favorite time was in the evening. My family worked hard, but after dinner, we walked to the park. The children played in the fountain, and the parents relaxed on the benches and talked about their day. It was fun because everyone was a friend or a relative.

B. Read the paragraphs in Activity A again. Underline the word before *park*, *fountain*, and *benches* each time. What do you see?

Word Partners

gather together

play together

work together

study together

live together

_____

GO ONLINE
to practice
word partners

the for second mention

After you introduce a singular, plural, or noncount noun and the reader knows about it, use *the* in front of the noun. *The* tells the reader that it is the same noun as the one you introduced before. *The* often appears in a supporting sentence.

Singular nouns

My family had <u>a big apartment</u> in the city. **The apartment** *was above a small shop.*

Noncount nouns

There was a lot of <u>traffic</u> at night. **The traffic** *was noisy, but we liked city life.*

Plural nouns

There were some <u>trees</u> outside our door. My brothers and I liked to climb **the trees** *after school.*

GO ONLINE for more practice

C. Read each sentence. Circle the letter of the best supporting sentence.

1. I walked to the corner shop to buy bread for my mother.

   a. Bread was hot and fresh.   b. The bread was hot and fresh.

2. My father had a big car.

   a. He used a car on long trips.   b. He used the car on long trips.

3. There was a park next to our building.

   a. The park had many benches and trees.   b. A park had many benches and trees.

4. My mother always gave us fruit.

   a. We ate fruit outside.   b. We ate the fruit outside.

D. Rewrite your paragraphs from page 67. Use the questions below to help you.

Oxford 2000

Do you need more words to write about your childhood community? Use the Oxford 2000 list on page 133 to find more words for your sentences.

Revising Questions

Can you:

- use *the* for second mention?
- use the Oxford 2000 to add more vocabulary words?
- add details?

Step 5 EDIT

A. Read the paragraphs below. Find and correct seven mistakes. The first mistake is corrected for you.

A Beach Community

My beautiful childhood home $\overset{was}{\wedge}$ in Nha Trang, Vietnam. There was a wide beach on one side of the city. My family had a restaurant near beach. We lived in a house behind restaurant. It always smelled like seafood and the ocean.

I worked a lot, but I enjoyed my free time. After lunch, I walk to the beach. My friends was there. We talked and play games. In the evening, I had to go back to restaurant, but it was a fun life. I enjoyed our beach community.

 B. Read your paragraphs again. Check (✓) the things in your paragraphs.

Editing Checklist

○ 1. Capital letters   ○ 2. *was* and *were*

○ 3. Periods   ○ 4. Descriptive details

○ 5. Simple past tense with *-ed* and *had*   ○ 6. *the* for second mention

 C. Now write your final paragraphs. Use the Editing Checklist to help you.

Step 6 PUBLISH

 Follow these steps to publish your paragraphs.

Publishing Steps

• Share your paragraphs with a partner.

• Answer the questions.

   • What sentence do you like in your partner's paragraphs?

   • What else do you want to know about your partner's childhood?

• Put your paragraphs in your portfolio!

Critical Thinking Question

What was your favorite thing about your childhood community? Explain.

- Use irregular past tense verbs
- Use the negative past tense with *did not*
- Use time expressions
- Use comparative adjectives
- Write paragraphs about how your city changed

▲ VOCABULARY ▸ Oxford 2000 ✎ words to talk about cities

A. Write the correct number from the pictures next to each item in the box.

_____ rode the bus to a sports stadium	_____ opened an international airport	1 a popular university landmark
_____ a train tunnel	_____ saves energy	_____ affected the economy
_____ a construction project		

B. Write each phrase below the correct picture.

affected the airport	took public transportation	improved a public park
a~~ government building~~	the energy business	international university students

1.

a government building

2.

3.

4.

5.

6.

Oxford 2000 🔑

Use the Oxford 2000 list on page 133 to find more words to describe the pictures on these pages. Share your words with a partner.

C. Circle the words that answer each question. You may circle more than one item.

1. Which are landmarks?   *a fountain   a government building   a bus   a park*

2. What does the government improve?   *streets   shops   rivers   public transportation*

3. What affects the economy?   *business   water   weather   sports*

4. What are projects?   *widening streets   planting trees   constructing schools   selling food*

5. What places are popular?   *parks   stadiums   hospitals   office buildings*

GO ONLINE for more practice

Vocabulary   71

▲▲ GRAMMAR
▶ Irregular past tense verbs
▶ Negative past tense with *did not*

A. Read Paulo's paragraphs. Why is the writer proud of his city?

A New Stadium

My city became famous because our football team was very good and won many championships. The city had a stadium downtown, but it was too small. The government decided to improve it. It spent a lot of money and built a better stadium. The project brought new business to the city.

Today, the stadium is popular because it is bigger and more beautiful. Tourists come to my city to enjoy the weather and the exciting sports events. They stay in the hotels by the beach and swim in the ocean during the day. At night, they go to the stadium and watch sports or other events. Our new football stadium is good for sports fans, and it also helps the local economy.

B. Read Paulo's first paragraph in Activity A again. Circle nine past tense verbs.

Grammar Note

Irregular past tense verbs
Some verbs are irregular in the simple past tense.

*After we **built** the stadium, the downtown **became** popular.*
*In the past, people **went** home for lunch.*

become ⟶ became   bring ⟶ brought   build ⟶ built
buy ⟶ bought   feel ⟶ felt   go ⟶ went
grow ⟶ grew   make ⟶ made   meet ⟶ met
spend ⟶ spent   take ⟶ took

GO ONLINE
for more
practice

Irregular past tense verbs stay the same for all subjects.

*The city **grew**.*   *The economy **grew**.*   *Trees **grew**.*

C. Read the paragraph below. Underline the irregular past tense verbs. Then write the past tense verbs next to the present tense verbs in the chart.

After our city <u>built</u> a park by the lake, people spent a lot of time there. They forgot about work and enjoyed nature. Many families brought their dinner and sat by the water. They ate and drank tea in the cool evening. Many people knew each other. Sometimes they rode bikes. People said hello and shared news. They felt good after the long, hot day.

Present	Irregular past tense
1. build	built
2. drink	
3. eat	
4. feel	
5. forget	
6. know	
7. say	
8. sit	
9. spend	
10. ride	
11. bring	

D. Choose one or two phrases from the box to complete each sentence. Add your own ideas. You do not have to use all of the phrases in the box.

brought business	made changes	spent money	became popular
went outside	built apartments	took pictures	grew strong

1. The economy grew strong, and people had jobs.

2. The government _____

3. The city _____

4. People _____

5. The new airport _____

6. Tourists _____

E. Use the words in the chart to write sentences.

The project became expensive.

The building The airport The project The city	became	busier more popular more international famous expensive
I Workers People Families	felt	happy safe good proud

GO ONLINE for more practice

Grammar Note

Negative past tense with *did not*
Use *did not* before the base form of the verb for something that was not true in the past.

Many years ago, my city was small.

> *The city **did not have** an airport.*
> *People **did not hurry**.*
> *The streets **did not feel** crowded.*

F. Write the letter of the phrase on the right to complete each sentence on the left.

1. __c__ The park did not have trees, so

2. ____ The city did not have an airport, so

3. ____ We did not bring food, so

4. ____ Many people went to the stadium, so

5. ____ Our street had a lot of traffic, so

6. ____ The project was difficult, so

a. we bought lunch at a café.

b. it took many years to finish.

c. ~~the city planted them.~~

d. the city built a tunnel for cars.

e. the downtown became more crowded when there was a game.

f. travelers rode the train.

G. Use each phrase to write about a time in the past. Change the verbs to the past tense or use *did not* + verb to write sentences.

1. have traffic

The streets did not have traffic.

2. have cell phones

_____

3. use computers

_____

4. eat in restaurants

_____

5. travel by airplane

_____

6. drive cars

_____

H. Circle the letter of the phrase that best completes each sentence.

1. The restaurants became popular because they

   a. had good food.

   b. did not have good food.

2. People were healthy because

   a. they had a place to get fresh air and exercise.

   b. they did not have a place to get fresh air and exercise.

3. The streets were quiet because

   a. the city had a lot of people.

   b. the city did not have a lot of people.

4. The new tunnel became a landmark because

   a. many people knew about the project.

   b. many people did not know about the project.

Chant

GO ONLINE
for the
Chapter 5
Vocabulary &
Grammar Chant

Writing Assignment What did your city build?

Cities grow and change. What did your city build? How did it affect the city or people?

Step 1 PREPARE

A. Read Maryam's paragraphs. How did construction change Dubai?

Desert City

In the past, Dubai was a quiet desert city, but it changed quickly. After international business came, the economy grew quickly. Dubai needed many new buildings, so businesspeople started many construction projects. Workers built shopping centers, office buildings, and big hotels. The city also opened universities, hospitals, and a new airport.

Now Dubai is a modern city. It is in a desert, but there are green parks, flower gardens, and large water fountains. There are many office buildings and the largest skyscraper in the world. People from different countries live here. They enjoy sports and fishing. At Ski Dubai, children play in the snow indoors. Dubai is interesting because it became a famous international city in a short time.

B. Answer the questions about the paragraphs in Activity A.

Paragraph 1: *What did Dubai build?*

1. What is Maryam's topic sentence? _____

2. What details explain the changes in Dubai?

_____

_____

Paragraph 2: *What is Dubai like now?*

3. What is Maryam's transition sentence? _____

4. What does Dubai look like now? _____

5. What do people do there? _____

6. How does Maryam feel about Dubai now? _____

Writing Strategy

Using time expressions

Writers help the reader understand a change in time by using time expressions.

Use *now* or *today* with a comma at the beginning of a sentence to show the present. Then use present tense verbs.

> **Today,** people <u>see</u> a lot of new construction downtown.

Use *in the past* or *many years ago* with a comma at the beginning of a sentence to show the past. Then use past tense verbs.

> **Many years ago,** people <u>visited</u> neighbors to get information.

GO ONLINE
for more
practice

C. Write one of the following time expressions at the beginning of each paragraph below. Some expressions may be used more than once.

> now   in the past   today   many years ago

1. _____Today,_____ many people live in cities. They shop in stores and buy their food, so they do not spend a lot of time outside.

   _____ many people lived in small communities. They worked outside. Families grew vegetables, and children took care of animals.

2. _____ people did not have cars. They walked and used bicycles to travel. The streets were small, and everyone knew their neighbors.

   _____ people have different choices. Some people walk or use a bicycle. Other people use cars or buses. They do not always know their neighbors in a big city.

3. _____ people move a lot. They get work in a new city, and they find a new home.

   _____ families stayed together and worked together. Children did not move. They lived with their parents.

Step 2 PREWRITE

A. Think of a city and circle things that the city built. Then choose one for your paragraph.

an airport	a hospital	a park	a building
a school or university	a stadium	other: _____	

B. Write a topic sentence and a transition sentence. Complete one of the sentences below or write your own sentences.

Topic sentence	Transition sentence
In the past,... did not have... Many years ago,... was... When I was a child, my city...	Now... is... Today,... has... Now... is different because...

C. Write notes about the past and the present.

The past	The present
The city:	The city:
People:	People:

Step 3 WRITE

A. Organize your paragraphs. Use your Prewrite notes to write sentences.

Paragraph 1: *What did your city build?*

1. What is your topic sentence? _____

2. What details from Prewrite do you want to include about the city and people in the past?

_____

_____

Paragraph 2: *What is your city like now?*

3. What is your transition sentence? _____

4. What details from Prewrite do you want to include about the city and people today?

_____

_____

5. How do you feel about the change? _____

Word Partners

grow bigger

grow quickly

grow vegetables

grow fruit

grow trees

grow up (in a city)

GO ONLINE
to practice
word partners

B. Use your sentences from Activity A to write two paragraphs. Add a title to your paragraphs.

Step 4 REVISE

A. Read David's paragraphs. What is an interesting thing about Taipei 101?

> # Taipei 101
>
> When Taiwan's economy grew, the city of Taipei built many new buildings. Many of them were special in different ways, but one project became famous internationally. That building was Taipei 101.
>
> Today, Taipei 101 is an important landmark. The construction is different from other buildings. It has 101 floors, so it is taller. Also, it is more beautiful. It has an Asian style, and every night the color changes. Taipei 101 is also safer in bad weather, and it saves energy. It is an example for other buildings, and people are proud of it.

B. Read the second paragraph in Activity A again. Circle *more* and the adjectives that end in -er.

Writing Strategy

Comparative adjectives
A short adjective with *-er* shows how one thing is different from another.

*We moved, and our new neighborhood is **quieter**. (compared to the old neighborhood)*

It can also show how one thing has changed.

*The town was small. Now it is **bigger**. (compared to the past)*

More goes in front of a long adjective. The adjective does not change.

*Many people moved to the area, and it became **more expensive**.*

The following words have spelling changes.

busy ⟶ busier   good ⟶ better

big ⟶ bigger   bad ⟶ worse

easy ⟶ easier

GO ONLINE
for more practice

C. Use comparative adjectives with *more* or *-er* to describe the pictures below. Write complete sentences.

Hotel A	Hotel B

Fullerton Hotel, Singapore	Marina Bay Sands Resort, Singapore

1. Hotel A is older. _____

2. _____

3. _____

4. _____

5. _____

6. _____

 D. Rewrite your paragraphs from page 79. Use the questions below to help you.

Oxford 2000 🔑

Do you need more words to write about what your city built? Use the Oxford 2000 list on page 133 to find more words for your sentences.

Revising Questions

Can you:

- use comparative adjectives to show differences?

- use the Oxford 2000 to add more vocabulary words?

- add details?

A. Read the paragraphs below. Find and correct eight mistakes. The first mistake is corrected for you.

Crossing the Bosphorus

Istanbul is a beautiful, historic city, but it has *a* problem. The Bosphorus River goes through the city, so some of the city is in Europe and some of the city is in Asia. In the past, people built bridges, but the city became busyier, and the bridges becomed crowded. People did not liked to wait in traffic. They needed a gooder way to go across the water.

The government not want to change the city, so it builted a train tunnel under the river. Now the Marmaray tunnel is helping people. It is easier for people to go to the other side of the river, and people save time. People are proud of the project. They have more fast transportation.

 B. Read your paragraphs again. Check (✓) the things in your paragraphs.

Editing Checklist

○ 1. Capital letters   ○ 2. Negative past tense with *did not*
○ 3. Periods   ○ 4. Time expressions
○ 5. Irregular past tense verbs   ○ 6. Comparative adjectives

 C. Now write your final paragraphs. Use the Editing Checklist to help you.

Step 6 **PUBLISH**

 Follow these steps to publish your paragraphs.

Publishing Steps

- Share your paragraphs with a partner.

- Answer the questions.

  - What is interesting about the changes in your partner's city?

  - Who do the changes affect?

- Put your paragraphs in your portfolio!

Critical Thinking Question

What do you want your city to build next? Why?

CHAPTER 6 — How Did a Place Surprise You?

- Use the past progressive
- Use adjective + infinitive
- Put background information before the topic sentence
- Use verbs with *that* in a conclusion
- Write paragraphs about a city experience

▲ VOCABULARY ▸ Oxford 2000 🔑 words to tell stories about experiences

A. Write the correct number from the pictures next to each item in the box.

__1__ explored the environment	____ snow blew in our faces	____ expected to see strange birds	____ a variety of plants
____ climbed some stairs	____ suddenly realized something	____ a tropical climate	____ shared memories
			____ the rainy season

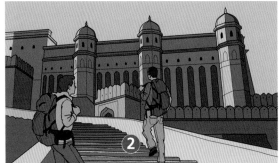

B. Write each phrase below the correct picture.

a cold climate	afraid of spiders	~~tropical fruit~~
get away from dangerous animals	a strange plant	noticed a friendly face

1.

tropical fruit

2.

_____

3.

_____

4.

_____

5.

_____

6.

_____

Oxford 2000 🔑

Use the Oxford 2000 list on page 133 to find more words to describe the pictures on these pages. Share your words with a partner.

C. Complete each sentence with a phrase from the box.

many stairs	beautiful birds	a variety of languages	~~cold weather~~

1. In winter, people want to get away from _____ cold weather _____.

2. In a tall building, people expect to climb _____.

3. In a tropical environment, people notice _____.

4. In a busy airport, people hear _____.

GO ONLINE
for more practice

A. Read Ana's paragraphs. What do you like about Ana's story?

Sumatra Story

Last year, my husband and I went to Sumatra in Indonesia for a vacation. We planned to see a lot of historic buildings and museums. We also wanted to take pictures of animals.

One afternoon while we were drinking Sumatran coffee, an old man joined our conversation. He told us about his childhood. He grew up in a tropical forest near tigers, but he was not afraid of them. He knew that birds always made noise when a dangerous animal was coming. He listened carefully to the birds while he was walking in the forest, and he got away from danger.

B. Check (✓) the picture that matches the paragraphs in Activity A.

Grammar Note

The past progressive
Use the past progressive to give background information in a story. To form the past progressive, use *was* or *were* with verb + *-ing*.

Sometimes the background information is a sentence by itself.

> I **was studying** in the library. Suddenly I heard a noise.

Sometimes the background information is in a sentence with *when*.

> Mr. Lee **was traveling** in Asia <u>when</u> he had an adventure on a river.

Sometimes the background information is in a sentence with *while* to show that an activity was interrupted.

> <u>While</u> we **were eating**, an old man walked up and asked for help.

GO ONLINE
for more
practice

C. Add background information to the sentences below by writing the letter of the correct sentence from the list.

a. Last year, I was coming home from the library.

b. While my sister and I were shopping, we met a lost child.

c. While my friend and I were walking on the beach, I noticed someone in the ocean.

d. One night, I was working late at the restaurant.

e. Mrs. Ma was driving me to a different city for a job.

f. The wind was blowing hard, and it was getting cold.

1. __c__ Suddenly he went under the water, and I realized that he needed help.

2. _____ Snow began to fall, and I knew that I had to find a place to get warm.

3. _____ She asked us to help her find her mother.

4. _____ Suddenly I saw one of my classmates. He was hurrying across the street.

5. _____ She was talking to me, and she did not see the animal on the street.

6. _____ A customer came in. I was serving his dinner when suddenly I realized that he was a famous musician.

D. Write background sentences for the stories below. Make past progressive sentences with *was* or *were* and words from the box.

living in Tokyo	driving in a strange city	visiting relatives
playing soccer	traveling in Kenya	waiting for the bus

1. _I was driving in a strange city._____ It started to rain. The streets became dangerous.

2. _____ We saw a dangerous animal. It was on the other side of the river.

3. _____ I met an old woman. She told me about her life.

4. _____ An old friend of the family came for tea. She introduced herself and told us a story about my father.

5. _____ I studied Japanese and became friends with my classmates.

6. _____ My friend was on my team, and he wanted to score a goal.

E. Read each pair of sentences. Change the first underlined verb to create background information. Write the sentence with *while* or *when*.

1. We <u>waited</u> for the server to bring our food.

    I <u>got</u> a text message.

    While we were waiting for the server to bring our food, I got a text message.

2. We <u>stood</u> in line.

    My father <u>stopped and pointed</u> at someone behind me.

    _____

3. My classmates and I <u>rode</u> the bus.

    Mr. Dinari <u>took</u> a picture.

    _____

4. We <u>look</u> for a hotel.

    The wind <u>blew</u> my map into the street.

    _____

5. My brother <u>traveled</u> to Los Angeles.

    He <u>met</u> a famous soccer player on the airplane.

    _____

6. My parents <u>walked</u> into the museum.

    They <u>saw</u> me.

    _____

Grammar Note

Adjective + infinitive

Use *it + is/was (not) + adjective + infinitive* to give an opinion about an activity.

> **It is important to visit** *Mr. Tanaka.*
>
> **It was nice to walk** *in the rain.*

To connect the idea to a person or people, add *for* + noun after the adjective.

> *It is* **hard for me** *to talk to new people.*
>
> *It was* **fun for my mother** *to visit relatives, so it was not easy to leave.*

GO ONLINE
for more
practice

F. Use the words in the chart to write sentences.

It is dangerous to go there.

| It | is (not)
was (not) | interesting
important
fun
hard
good
dangerous | to see
to experience
to enjoy | a strange city
new people
nature |
| | | | to go
to take pictures
to walk | there
at night
in the forest |

G. Read the sentences with a partner. Check (✓) the boxes that you and your partner agree with.

	Me	My partner	Both of us
1. It is nice to have pictures of my travels.			
2. It is fun to see new cities.			
3. It is hard to sleep in a new place.			
4. It is fun to watch soccer.			
5. It is important to visit relatives.			
6. It is easy to meet people.			

H. Rewrite each sentence from Activity G below. Add *for me, for her, for him,* or *for us*. Make other necessary changes.

1. *It is nice for us to have pictures of our travels.*

2. _____

3. _____

4. _____

5. _____

6. _____

Chant

GO ONLINE
for the
Chapter 6
Vocabulary &
Grammar Chant

▲▲▲ **WRITING**
▶ Putting background information before the topic sentence
▶ Verb with *that* in a conclusion

Writing Assignment How did a place surprise you?

Every city is special in some way. Write about a city experience. Tell a story. What did you expect to happen, and what happened?

Step 1 PREPARE

A. Read Phuong's paragraphs. What surprised her?

A Winter Memory

I grew up in a tropical climate. In Vietnam, we had a rainy season and a dry season. I enjoyed the rain. It made a lot of noise, and it had a special smell. I knew a lot about rain, but I never experienced snow. Then one winter, my family went to Amsterdam, the Netherlands, to visit my brother. I expected to see museums and experience cold weather, but the winter snow was a surprise.

My brother met us at the airport. When we walked outside, the wind was blowing. I was wearing warm clothes, but I was cold. We rode the train to the city. When we got off, it was snowing. The snow was soft and slow. I felt surprised because it was quiet. I did not expect that. In Vietnam, the rain is noisy, but I realized that snow does not make noise.

B. Answer the questions about the paragraphs in Activity A.

Paragraph 1: *What did Phuong expect, and why?*

1. What was Phuong's background? _____

2. Phuong says she knew about rain but not snow. Why was it important for her to say that? _____

3. What did she expect in the new city? _____

4. What is her topic sentence? _____

Paragraph 2: *What happened?*

5. What is the transition sentence? Does it start the paragraph well?

_____

6. What details does Phuong tell in her story to help the reader understand the

experience? _____

7. What did she learn, and why do you think it was a surprise?

_____

Writing Strategy

Putting background information before the topic sentence
Sometimes writers give background information before the topic sentence.
Background information shows why the main idea is important.

*I spent my childhood in the mountains. I knew a lot about the mountains and I
enjoyed my life, but I did not know anything about big cities.* **The first time I
went to a city was an adventure.**

> The story is more interesting because now
> the reader knows that the writer's story is
> about seeing the city for the first time.

GO ONLINE
for more
practice

**C. Read the paragraphs below. Choose the best topic sentence for the end of the
first paragraph and circle it. Then write it on the line.**

> Last year, I went to Houston, Texas, for a business trip. My friends said
> that Houston was not a beautiful city. They said that it was always hot. They
> complained about all the traffic. _____
>
> I was staying in a hotel near downtown, and one day I walked to a park.
> I followed the sidewalk to a river. People were walking by the river. Some
> children were riding bicycles across a bridge. It was green and beautiful. I
> learned that Houston is a nice place to visit.

Topic sentence: a. I was not happy because I wanted to leave Houston.

b. My friends did not like Houston, and they did not want
   me to go.

c. I did not expect to like Houston, but I was surprised.

A. Think about cities you lived in or visited. Fill in the chart with the names of cities that surprised you.

Feature	Name of city
1. a strange climate	
2. interesting people	
3. historic buildings and streets	
4. beautiful parks and nature	
5. busy traffic	
6. sports and activities	

B. Write a topic sentence. Complete one of the sentences below or write your own sentence.

Topic sentence
I saw many things, but did not expect to see...   I was surprised because...   I had many interesting experiences, but one experience surprised me.

C. Think about ideas for the different parts of your paragraphs. Write your ideas in the chart below.

Paragraph 1
Where did you go? Why?

What background information do you want to share?

What did you expect?

Paragraph 2
What happened that surprised you?

What did you do?

What did you see?

How did you feel?

Step 3 WRITE

A. Organize your paragraphs. Use your Prewrite notes to write sentences.

Paragraph 1: *What did you expect, and why?*

1. What do you want to explain about yourself or your trip? _____

2. What background information from Prewrite is important?

_____

_____

3. What is your topic sentence? _____

Paragraph 2: *What happened?*

4. What is the first thing that happened in your story? _____

5. What details from Prewrite do you want to include about the place, the weather, and the things that you saw or experienced?

_____

_____

Word Partners

a variety of people

a variety of plants

a variety of fruits and vegetables

a variety of museums

GO ONLINE
to practice
word partners

B. Use your sentences from Activity A to write two paragraphs. Add a title to your paragraphs.

Step 4 REVISE

A. Read Christa's paragraphs. Why was the place beautiful and strange?

The Highline

When I first came to the United States, I went to New York. I expected to see a modern city with tall buildings, famous museums, and fashionable stores. When I went there, I explored the city environment, and I learned that New York also had some strange and beautiful outdoor places.

One day, I was walking in the city, and I got lost. While I was looking at my map, a woman helped me. She told me to visit the Highline, and she showed me some stairs. I went up and saw a long sidewalk with trees and plants. People were walking and sitting on benches. I explored and took a lot of pictures. I realized that it was a nice way to experience the city.

B. Read the paragraphs in Activity A again. Underline the sentences with *I learned that* and *I realized that.*

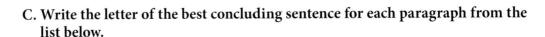

Writing Strategy

Verbs with *that* in a conclusion

In a concluding sentence, use a verb + *that* before a subject to show how you learned something. *Learned, noticed, realized, knew,* and *understood* are often used with *that.*

> I **learned that** snow is quiet.
> We suddenly **realized that** we had a family connection.
> He **knew that** he was in the wrong place.

GO ONLINE
for more
practice

C. Write the letter of the best concluding sentence for each paragraph from the list below.

a.   We learned that it is important to experience new food.

b.   I understood that a little danger is fun.

c.   He realized that many of his friends were not living there.

d.   ~~We knew that we wanted to go back to Paris.~~

1. When we got back to the hotel, we felt tired. There were many museums, but we did not see all of them. __d__

2. I was happy because I was safe. I enjoyed the adventure in the mountains. _____

3. We ate a lot of strange food on that trip. There were many good restaurants in Beijing, and we tried many things. _____

4. When he came back to Jakarta, he wanted to visit his childhood neighbors, but the neighborhood was different. _____

 D. Rewrite your paragraphs from page 91. Use the questions below to help you.

Oxford 2000 🔑

Do you need more words to write about how a place surprised you? Use the Oxford 2000 list on page 133 to find more words for your sentences.

Revising Questions

Can you:

• use verbs with *that*?

• use the Oxford 2000 to add more vocabulary words?

• add details?

A. Read the paragraphs below. Find and correct six mistakes. The first mistake is corrected for you.

Santiago Culture

My mother is from Santiago, Chile. Our family visited her family last

expected

summer. I ~~expecting~~ to see beautiful mountains, and I was right. There

were many mountains, but I also learn that the culture was interesting.

Our relatives showed us museums, and they told us about their

history. It was interesting learn about Chile. I realized that there a lot of

art in the city. People also liked to read. It was important them to have

books. There were small bookshops on the streets, and many people were

wait in lines to get books. My mother was proud of her city.

B. Read your paragraphs again. Check (✓) the things in your paragraphs.

Editing Checklist

○ 1. Capital letters   ○ 2. The past progressive

○ 3. Periods   ○ 4. Adjective + infinitive

○ 5. Irregular past tense verbs   ○ 6. Verbs with *that* in a conclusion

---

C. Now write your final paragraphs. Use the Editing Checklist to help you.

Step 6 PUBLISH

Follow these steps to publish your paragraphs.

Publishing Steps

- Share your paragraphs with a partner.

- Answer the questions.

  - What did your partner's experience make you realize?

  - Why do you think your partner was surprised?

- Put your paragraphs in your portfolio!

Critical Thinking Question

What surprises people when they visit your city?

Extend Your Skills

Look at the word bank for Unit 2. Check (✓) the words you know. Circle the words you want to learn better.

OXFORD 2000 🔑

Adjectives	Nouns			Verbs
afraid	airport	energy	season	affect
dangerous	animal	environment	snow	blow
downstairs	bridge	face	stair	build
healthy	bus	government	traffic	expect
international	business	group	train	explore
local	childhood	home	transportation	get (away)
noisy	climate	memory	tunnel	hurry
public	corner	park	university	improve
strange	danger	plant	variety	join
strong	economy	project		live (in)
wide				notice
				realize
				save

PRACTICE WITH THE OXFORD 2000 🔑

A. Use the words in the chart. Match adjectives with nouns.

1. _international airport_   2. _____

3. _____   4. _____

5. _____   6. _____

B. Use the words in the chart. Match verbs with nouns.

1. _explore a park_   2. _____

3. _____   4. _____

5. _____   6. _____

C. Use the words in the chart. Match verbs with adjective noun partners.

1. _affect the local environment_   2. _____

3. _____   4. _____

5. _____   6. _____

UNIT **3** Lifestyles

Who Are 21st-Century Teenagers?

- Use *used to* + verb
- Use *more/less* + noun
- Use *instead*

- Use *more/less* + long adjective
- Write paragraphs comparing teenagers in the past and today

▲ VOCABULARY ► Oxford 2000 🔑 words to talk about how teenagers behave

A. Write the correct number from the pictures next to each item in the box.

_____ explores imaginary worlds with friends	_____ went fishing in our free time	_____ does not concentrate on his chores
_____ share secrets	_____ rode motorcycles	_____ communicate by text
_1_ hangs out online		

B. Write each phrase below the correct picture.

| an imaginary tree | spend time fishing | an old village |
| prefer to ride motorcycles | various chores | a 21st-century farm |

1.

prefer to ride motorcycles

2.

3.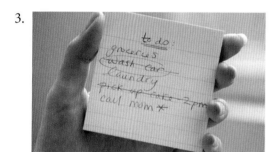

4.

5.

6.

Oxford 2000 🔑

Use the Oxford 2000 list on page 133 to find more words to describe the pictures on these pages. Share your words with a partner.

C. Write each word or phrase from the first column before or after the words in the second and third columns to make phrases.

1. hang out   hang out online   usually hang out

2. go   fishing   outside

3. secrets   share   family

4. teenagers   21st-century   young

5. life   social   skills

6. world   small   imaginary

7. time   have   free

GO ONLINE for more practice

A. Read the paragraphs. Who is writing the paragraphs?

Two Different Worlds

When I was a young teenager, I had an active social life. I made plans with friends every day. After school, my friends and I used to hang out together. Sometimes we walked around the city and listened to musicians. In the summer, we met at the local beach and went fishing. We knew our city well, and we did not spend a lot of time at home.

Today, teenagers' social lives are changing. They are spending less time together in the real world. Instead, they prefer to go online. For example, my son is fourteen, and he plays a lot of video games. He meets his school friends online, and they build imaginary environments together. In the summer, he likes to stay home and text his friends. I think that modern technology is making him experience the world differently.

B. Read each statement about the paragraphs in Activity A. Write *T* (true) or *F* (false).

_____ 1. The writer spent his teenage days outside.

_____ 2. The writer used to listen to music in the city.

_____ 3. The writer used to go to the beach after school.

_____ 4. The son prefers to communicate online.

_____ 5. The son understands modern technology.

Grammar Note

used to + verb

Use *used to* + verb to explain that something was true in the past but is not true now.

I **used to work** on my grandfather's farm. My brother **used to take care** of the animals.

We **used to hang out** at the beach on weekends.

Teenagers **used to read** more books, but now they watch videos online.

GO ONLINE
for more
practice

C. Read the sentences. Fill in each blank with *used to* + a verb from the box.

be	communicate	share
clean	learn	take

1. My father did not text his friends when he was young. They
   used to communicate by phone.

2. My mother _____ my room, but now she just closes the door.

3. Today, I prefer to drive, but I _____ the train.

4. My daughter _____ her secrets with me, but now she tells
   them to her friends.

5. Teenagers _____ from books, but now they prefer to use
   technology.

6. She _____ shy, but now she has an active social life.

D. Use the words in the chart to write sentences.

In the past, children used to have more free time.

In the past,	I	used to	be more adventurous
	my friends		communicate differently
	children		do more chores
	we		go to bed early
	teenagers		go fishing
			have more free time
			spend more time outside
			wake up late

1. _____

2. _____

3. _____

4. _____

5. _____

more/less + noun

Use *more* with plural count nouns and noncount nouns to show that the amount of something has increased.

> *Our community needs **more trees**.*
>
> *I have **more fun** at home.*

Use *less* with noncount nouns to show that the amount of something has decreased.

> *My son has **less time** outside.*
>
> *Teenagers today get **less information** from books.*

GO ONLINE
for more practice

E. Circle the letter of the phrase that best completes each sentence. Then write the correct sentence.

1. I am busy, so

   a. I have less time to read.   b. I have more free time.

   I am busy, so I have less time to read.

2. My city is growing, so

   a. there is less public transportation.   b. there are more buildings.

   _____

3. 21st-century teenagers like to text, so

   a. they spend less money.   b. they spend more time on their phones.

   _____

4. I lived on a busy street, so

   a. there was more danger.   b. there was less energy.

   _____

5. Many people ride bicycles in my neighborhood, so

   a. it has less traffic.   b. it has more cars.

   _____

6. Our village was small, so

   a. there were more businesses.   b. there was less variety.

   _____

F. Give your opinion about teenagers. Write sentences with *in the past* or *today* and the sentence cues below.

1. teenagers / do / more schoolwork

Today, teenagers do more schoolwork.

2. teenagers / spend / less time outside

_____

3. teenagers / have / more imagination

_____

4. teenagers / use / less technology

_____

5. teenagers / have / closer connections with their local community

_____

6. teenagers / know / more information about the world

_____

7. teenagers / spend / less time online

_____

8. teenagers / understand / more about other cultures

_____

Chant

GO ONLINE
for the
Chapter 7
Vocabulary &
Grammar Chant

Writing Assignment Who are 21st-century teenagers?

Teenagers' lives are changing quickly in the 21st century. What were teenagers like in the past? How are teenagers different today?

Step 1 PREPARE

A. Read the paragraphs. Why does the writer talk about his father?

My Father and Me

My family used to live on a farm in a small village. When my father was a teenager, he had various chores to do. He used to wake up early, and he took care of the animals. He gave them water and food, and he kept them healthy. His days on the farm were long, but his secret to success was working hard.

Today, teenagers do not work on the farms. Instead, they are learning about technology. Their parents want them to concentrate on their education, so they do more work on computers. My father wants me to go to a good university, so I study hard. I realize that my world is different, but I respect my father and want him to be proud of me.

B. Answer the questions about the paragraphs in Activity A.

Paragraph 1: *teenagers in the past*

1. Where did the writer's father grow up? _____ _____

2. What did his father do as a teenager? _____

3. What is the writer's topic sentence? _____

Paragraph 2: *teenagers today*

4. What is the writer's transition sentence? _____

5. How are teenagers' lives different today? _____

6. What does the writer realize? _____

A. Compare differences between teenagers in the past and today. Then choose which ideas you want to use in your paragraphs.

	In the past	Today
1. how teenagers spend time	played outside	
2. how they communicate		
3. what they concentrate on		
4. how they learn		
5. what they think		

B. Write a topic sentence and a transition sentence. Complete one of the sentences below or write your own sentences.

Topic sentence	Transition sentence
When I was a teenager, I… My parents were… I think teenagers used to…	I think 21st-century teenagers… Now, teenagers have more/less… Today, my teenage son/ daughter…

C. Think about ideas for the different parts of your paragraphs. Write your ideas in the chart below.

Teenagers in the past	Teenagers today
What were teenagers like in the past? What did they do?	What are 21st-century teenagers like? How are their lives different?

Step 3 WRITE

A. Organize your paragraphs. Use your Prewrite notes to write sentences.

Paragraph 1: *teenagers in the past*

1. What is your topic? _____

2. What details from Prewrite do you want to include?

_____

_____

3. What is your topic sentence? _____

Paragraph 2: *teenagers today*

4. What is your transition sentence? _____

5. What details from Prewrite do you want to include?

_____

_____

6. What do you realize about the differences? _____

Word Partners

a different world

an imaginary world

a small world

the modern world

the real world

GO ONLINE
to practice
word partners

 B. Use your sentences from Activity A to write two paragraphs. Add a title to your paragraphs.

Step 4 REVISE

A. Read the paragraphs. What is the writer's opinion about teenagers today?

Learning from Us

My parents did not grow up with computers. Instead, they got information from books and newspapers, and they spent more time in libraries. They knew about their country's history, but they did not focus on other places. They were not less intelligent, but I think that their world was smaller.

I think that 21st-century teenagers have more knowledge about the world. We watch a lot of videos on the Internet and see more international news. We do not just concentrate on our nation. Instead, we explore many cultures. We experience more variety, and our world feels bigger.

B. Read the paragraphs in Activity A again. Circle *instead*.

instead

Instead shows a relationship between two sentences. Use *instead* to explain a different situation or choice. Put a comma after *instead*.

> *My parents did not have the Internet.* **Instead***, they got information from books.*
> *I pay less attention to sports now.* **Instead***, I concentrate on school.*

GO ONLINE
for more
practice

C. Check (✓) the sentences that use *instead* correctly.

__✓__ 1. I did not have a lot of free time. Instead, I had many responsibilities.

_____ 2. My parents never went to college. Instead, they worked.

_____ 3. Our city is improving transportation. Instead, it is building a new airport.

_____ 4. Teenagers spend less time together. Instead, they hang out online.

D. Use each set of phrases to write a sentence about yourself. Use *instead*.

1. ride the bus / drive to school

I do not ride the bus. Instead, I drive to school.

2. like busy cities / enjoy quiet villages

_____

3. communicate by text / prefer conversations by phone

_____

4. like to be social / enjoy time alone

_____

E. Rewrite your paragraphs from page 104. Use the questions below to help you.

Revising Questions

Can you:

- use *instead* to show a difference?
- use the Oxford 2000 to add more vocabulary words?
- add details?

Oxford 2000 🔑

Do you need more words to write about 21st-century teenagers? Use the Oxford 2000 list on page 133 to find more words for your sentences.

Writing Strategy

more/less + long adjective

In Chapter 5, you learned that writers use *more* with long adjectives to show a change. Long adjectives have two or more syllables.

> *Teenagers today are* **more active** *online.* (2 syllables: ac • tive)
>
> *A university education is* **more important** *today.* (3 syllables: im • por • tant)

To describe how something has decreased, use *less* with long adjectives.

> *Teenagers' lives were* **less difficult** *in the past.*
>
> *I like small villages because they are* **less noisy**.

GO ONLINE
for more
practice

A. Read the paragraphs. Then write sentences about each sister. Use *more* and *less* with adjectives to compare the sisters.

My Teenage Sisters

I have two teenage sisters, but they enjoy different experiences. Xuan has many friends, and they are always together. They like to spend time in the city. They ride their motorcycles on busy streets downtown. It is dangerous because there is usually a lot of traffic. Sometimes Xuan comes home late, and my parents get angry because she forgets to text.

My sister Tuyen has a quieter life. She knows a lot of people, but she does not have many friends because she is shy and she is happier alone. She prefers to stay home and read books. She has a good imagination, and she writes stories in her free time. In the evening, she helps around the house. My parents are busy, so Tuyen often cooks dinner and cleans for them.

1. Xuan / active   *Xuan is more active.* _____

2. Xuan / friendly   _____

3. Xuan / responsible   _____

4. Tuyen / social   _____

5. Tuyen / adventurous   _____

6. Tuyen / serious   _____

B. Read the paragraphs below. Find and correct eight mistakes. The first mistake is corrected for you.

From Fashion to Sports

used to

When I was a teenager, I liked fashion. After school, I ~~use to~~ go shopping downtown with my friends. We get ideas from famous people and magazines, and we shared fashion secret. We wanted people to pay attention to us, so we try to dress differently. Sometimes our clothes looked strange, but we did not mind.

Now I am older, and I have a teenage daughter. I still buy a lot of clothes, but fashion is lesser important to my daughter, instead, she enjoys sports, and she is more adventure. She and her friends do not go shopping on weekends. Instead they go mountain climbing or play soccer.

 C. Read your paragraphs again. Check (✓) the things in your paragraphs.

Editing Checklist

○ 1. Capital letters ○ 2. *more/less* + noun

○ 3. Periods ○ 4. *instead*

○ 5. *used to* + verb ○ 6. *more/less* + long adjective

 D. Now write your final paragraphs. Use the Editing Checklist to help you.

Step 6 PUBLISH

 Follow these steps to publish your paragraphs.

Publishing Steps

• Share your paragraphs with a partner.

• Answer the questions.

  • Which ideas do you find interesting?

  • Do you agree or disagree with your partner? Why?

• Put your paragraphs in your portfolio!

Critical Thinking Question

What skills do teenagers need to be successful in the modern world?

CHAPTER 8

What Does Your Future Look Like?

- Use *will (not)* + verb
- Use *can* + verb
- Use *maybe* and *then*

- Use gerunds after prepositions
- Write paragraphs explaining a career path

▲ VOCABULARY ▶ Oxford 2000 🔑 words to describe career paths

A. Write the correct number from the pictures next to each item in the box.

—— a successful career with a sports team

—— make a decision

—— become a businessperson

—— a medical degree

1 a job in science

—— solve a problem

—— a traffic engineer

—— get a college education

B. Circle the correct words to describe each picture.

1.

face an engineering challenge

face a business challenge

2.

an opportunity to help people

an opportunity to design clothes

3.

a quick solution

an expensive solution

4.

a creative education

a creative design

5.

achieve a goal

achieve a win

6.

provide a medical solution

provide a place to work

Oxford 2000

Use the Oxford 2000 list on page 133 to find more words to describe the pictures on these pages. Share your words with a partner.

C. Check (✓) the careers. Some will have more than one check.

People with this job...	Computer Science	Engineering	Medicine	Sports	Fashion
1. find solutions to problems.					
2. provide services to people.					
3. design new products.					
4. need a college degree.					

GO ONLINE
for more practice

A. Read the paragraphs. Do you think the writer has a good plan? Explain.

Fun in Education

I think about my future a lot. I hope to live in a big city and work for a software company because I like computers and technology, and I am good at working on a team. My coworkers and I will face important challenges, and maybe we will argue, but we will find creative solutions together.

I have a plan to achieve my goal. I think that education will change in the future, so I want to focus on designing fun, educational games. Teenagers and children prefer to learn online, so I think there will be many opportunities. First, I will get a degree in computer science. Then I will design new games and show them to companies. Maybe I will be successful, and I can make a difference in the world.

B. Read the sentences about the paragraphs in Activity A. Check (✓) the sentences that are true about the writer.

___✓___ 1. She hopes that she will work with computers.

_____ 2. In her future job, she will work with other people.

_____ 3. She will not live in a big city.

_____ 4. She believes that learning can be fun.

_____ 5. She thinks that the future will be different.

_____ 6. She hopes that her work will help people.

will (not) + verb

Use *will (not)* before a verb to write about the future.

> In my future career, I **will travel** around the world.

> In the future, speaking English **will not be** difficult for me.

Use *will* before *be* with adjectives and nouns.

> The new software **will be popular** with teenagers.

> My brother **will be an engineer** next year.

GO ONLINE
for more practice

C. Use the timeline to write a paragraph about Mona.

go to college	earn a degree in fashion design	get a job with a famous designer	learn about the business	save money	start her own company

Mona will go to college. _____

_____

_____

_____

D. Use the words in the chart to write sentences.

My coworkers will be good at solving problems.

I My coworkers My classmates My work team	will (not)	explore career opportunities study languages learn about business be patient be hardworking be good at solving problems
My job My life My work	will (not)	be boring be difficult be fun be challenging

can + verb

Use *can* + verb to describe opportunities and skills that are true now.

*I **can solve** math problems.*

*I **can walk** to work because I live near the building.*

Use *can* + verb to describe opportunities and skills that will be true in the future.

*I study English so in the future I **can work** for an international company.*

*I want to save money so I **can buy** a car.*

When you use two verbs, use *can* one time.

*I **can travel** and **meet** new people.*

*We **can meet** for lunch and **talk** about business.*

GO ONLINE
for more
practice

E. Complete each sentence with a phrase from the box.

help children learn	buy a big house	help people with medical problems
make beautiful clothes	open a restaurant	walk to work

1. I hope to get a degree in business. Then I can *open a restaurant.* _____

2. I want to make a lot of money. Then I can _____

3. I hope to become a doctor. Then I can _____

4. I want to be a fashion designer. Then I can _____

5. I expect to live in an apartment in the city. Then I can _____

6. I will get a job in a school. Then I can _____

F. Circle two phrases that answer each question. Then write sentences with *can*. There is more than one right answer.

1. What can a salesperson do?

   sell products   *help customers*   *talk about prices*

   A salesperson can help customers and sell products.

2. What can a doctor do?

   listen to patients   *solve medical problems*   *help people*

   _____

3. What can a computer scientist do?

   design software   *understand computer languages*   *solve difficult problems*

   _____

4. What can an engineer do?

   solve building problems   *design tunnels*   *build bridges*

   _____

5. What can a teacher do?

   explain problems   *help students*   *give directions*

   _____

6. What can a businessperson do?

   sell clothes   *talk to customers*   *open a restaurant*

   _____

Chant

GO ONLINE for the Chapter 8 Vocabulary & Grammar Chant

Writing Assignment What does your future look like?

Education helps people accomplish future goals. How do you imagine your future life? How will education help you achieve your goals?

Step 1 PREPARE

A. Read Juan's paragraphs. Do you think he is making a good choice?

Opportunities in Sports

When I imagine my future life, I ask myself a question: What do I like? My answer is sports. I spend a lot of time at the local stadium, and the games are always exciting. In my favorite games, I expect my team to lose, but they try hard and score a goal. Then I feel good all day. Sports will always be popular, so I think there will be good opportunities in the sports business.

I have a plan for my education. I can study business and get experience in sales. Then I will try to get a job with a sports team. I have good social skills, so maybe I can sell advertising or work with players to advertise products for companies. I can travel with the team, make money, and watch games at stadiums around the world.

B. Answer the questions about the paragraphs in Activity A.

Paragraph 1: *How does Juan imagine his future life?*

1. What do you learn about Juan's interests? _____

2. What does Juan like about sports? How do you know? _____

_____

3. What is Juan's conclusion about his future? _____

Paragraph 2: *How will education and/or experience help him achieve his goals?*

4. What is the transition sentence? _____

5. What is Juan's plan? _____

6. What other skills does he have? _____ _____

7. What does Juan expect to do in the future? _____

GO ONLINE
for more
practice

Writing Strategy

maybe and *then*

Maybe is often used with *can* and *will* to show that something is not definite. The writer is exploring different ideas or future possibilities.

> **Maybe** I **will** become an engineer.
>
> **Maybe** our ideas **can** change the world.

Use *then* to show that something happens after a first event or action. There is usually a relationship between the two events.

Time relationship:

> *I will study English.* **Then** *I will study science.*

Result relationship:

> *I will get a degree.* **Then** *I can get a better job.*

Use *maybe* and *then* before the subject. Do not use a comma.

C. Read the sentences. Write *then* or *maybe* in each blank.

1. I have a plan for the future. First, I will work and save money. _____Then_____ I will go to college. I do not want to study and work at the same time.

2. I need to make a decision, but it is hard to choose one career. I like the idea of working in a store. _____ I will study business.

3. It is not easy to make a decision about a career. First, I plan to take different classes in college. _____ I will decide.

4. I like children, and I want to be a teacher. First, I will help teachers in their classrooms. _____ I will have experience, and I can work in my own classroom.

5. I am interested in working in a hotel. I will learn other languages in college. _____ I can talk to guests from different countries.

6. I like shopping for clothes, and my friends think that I know a lot about fashion. _____ I can work for a clothing store in the future.

Step 2 PREWRITE

A. Use the organizer to explore your interests and educational opportunities.

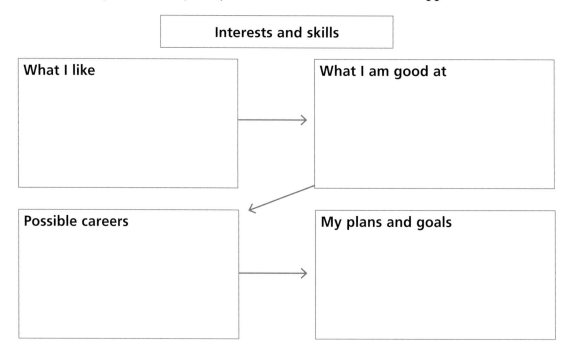

B. Write a topic sentence and a transition sentence. Complete one of the sentences below or write your own sentences.

Topic sentence	Transition sentence
I like…	There are many jobs connected to…
My family expects me to…	I am good at…, so I want to…
When I imagine my future, I think about…	It is hard to decide on a career, but I want to work with…

Step 3 WRITE

A. Organize your paragraphs. Use your Prewrite notes to write sentences.

Paragraph 1: *How do you imagine your future life?*

1. What is your topic sentence? _____

2. What details about your interests do you want to include?

_____

_____

Paragraph 2: *How will education and/or experience help you achieve your goals?*

3. What is your transition sentence? _____

4. What details about your educational goals do you want to include?

_____

_____

5. What will you feel or do when you have this job?

_____

Word Partners

provide
opportunities

provide a solution

provide information

provide a way (to)

provide a place (to)

———————————

GO ONLINE
to practice
word partners

✎ **B. Use your sentences from Activity A to write two paragraphs. Add a title to your paragraphs.**

Step 4 REVISE

A. Read the paragraphs. Why did the writer change careers?

A Career with Plants

In the past, I expected to be a doctor. My parents always wanted my sister and me to study medicine. When they came to the United States 20 years ago, they worked hard to pay for our education. I was interested in studying science, but I did not like hospitals. I realized that I wanted to work outside in nature, so I changed my educational goal.

I am good at working with plants, and I like beautiful gardens, so I plan to study park design. I will learn about creating beautiful and healthy outdoor places. In the future, I will use my skills to design and improve parks, streets, and businesses. My sister will be a doctor, but I am looking forward to helping people in a different way.

B. Read the paragraphs in Activity A again. Circle the prepositions *in, at,* and *about* and the *-ing* words that follow them.

Gerunds after prepositions

Use a gerund (verb + -ing) after a preposition when you want to use a verb as a noun.

*I am excited **about helping** patients.*

Prepositions with nouns	Prepositions with gerunds
I look forward to college.	*I look forward **to learning** about history.*
I am interested in business.	*I am interested **in working** for a big company.*
I am good at math.	*I am good **at solving** problems.*

GO ONLINE
for more
practice

C. Read each sentence. Fill in the blank with a phrase from the box.

working with trees	designing bridges	improving safety
achieving a goal	telling stories	selling plants

1. I enjoy a challenge. I am excited about _____ *achieving a goal* _____.

2. I like to learn about nature. I am interested in _____.

3. My father is an engineer. He is good at _____.

4. I plan to have a gardening business. I look forward to _____.

5. She wants to be a writer because she is good at _____.

6. I want to work for the city. I am excited about _____.

 D. Rewrite your paragraphs from page 117. Use the questions below to help you.

Oxford 2000

Do you need more words to write about your career path? Use the Oxford 2000 list on page 133 to find more words for your sentences.

Revising Questions

Can you:

- use *maybe* or *then* to explain your ideas better?
- use the Oxford 2000 to add more vocabulary words?
- add details?

A. Read the paragraphs below. Find and correct six mistakes. The first mistake is corrected for you.

A Life in the Classroom

    I am interested in ~~work~~ *working* with children. I have good memories of my childhood, and I believe that I can provide good experiences for other children. I will to face many challenge before I achieve my goal, but I think I can become a teacher.

    I plan to take English classes. Then I can to teach in an international school. I look forward to work with kids from all over the world. I will giving them opportunities to learn math and science, and I will help them become creative. I will need a lot of energy, but I will like this job.

 B. Read your paragraphs again. Check (✓) the things in your paragraphs.

Editing Checklist

○ 1. Capital letters   ○ 2. *maybe* and *then*

○ 3. Periods   ○ 4. Gerunds after prepositions

○ 5. *will (not)* and *can* + verb

C. Now write your final paragraphs. Use the Editing Checklist to help you.

 Follow these steps to publish your paragraphs.

Publishing Steps

- Share your paragraphs with a partner.
- Answer the questions.
  - What did you learn about your partner's skills?
  - What do you think about your partner's future job?
- Put your paragraphs in your portfolio!

Critical Thinking Question

Do you know someone who made a good or bad decision when choosing a career? Explain.

Who Is Your Country Proud Of?

- Use *could (not)* + verb
- Use *so that*
- Use *also*

- Use verbs followed by gerunds
- Write paragraphs about an important person from your country

▲ VOCABULARY

▶ Oxford 2000 🔑 words to talk about important people from your country

A. Write the correct number from the pictures next to each item in the box.

—— films about powerful characters	—— continued painting all her life	—— a filmmaker	—— a photography museum
—— painted pretty images of nature	—— appreciate a famous artist	*1* improve the environment	—— created original fashion designs
		—— provide help	

B. Write each phrase below the correct picture.

a black-and-white photograph	~~an art museum~~	a strange environment
community support	protect trees	a talented painter

1.

___an art museum___

2.

_____

3.

_____

4.

_____

5.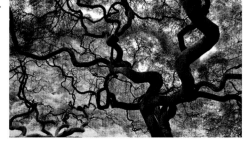

_____

6.

_____

Oxford 2000 🔑

Use the Oxford 2000 list on page 133 to find more words to describe the pictures on these pages. Share your words with a partner.

C. Match the people to what they do.

__e__ 1. artists

_____ 2. filmmakers

_____ 3. musicians

_____ 4. painters

_____ 5. photographers

_____ 6. writers

_____ 7. engineers

a. design buildings

b. make paintings

c. make movies

d. write stories

e. ~~do creative things~~

f. play music

g. take pictures

GO ONLINE
for more practice

A. Read the paragraphs. How did Wangari Maathai help people?

Wangari Maathai

Wangari Maathai helped her country. She grew up in a small village in Kenya. When she was older, she realized that many villages did not have enough trees. She taught women to grow young trees and take care of them. The trees collected water for the land and the farms, and they also provided more wood for homes. Women could grow more vegetables, and they made money so that they could support their families.

Maathai did not just plant trees. She also made Kenyan women proud of their new skills. Many women could not imagine themselves growing trees, but she believed in them. They appreciated her hard work, and they felt good about improving their environment. Today, she is famous because other countries use her ideas. Because of Maathai, there are millions of new trees around the world.

B. Check (✓) the picture that matches the paragraphs in Activity A.

Grammar Note

could (not) + verb

Use *could* + verb to say that something was able to happen in the past.

> Maathai **could solve** the problem because she had the support of the local community.
> There was more water, so the women **could plant** vegetables.

Use *could not* to show the negative.

> The land **could not support** farming because it was dry.
> The women **could not understand** how to grow trees without her help.

GO ONLINE for more practice

C. Finish each sentence with *could* and the words in parentheses.

1. The engineer was famous because he *could design modern buildings.*

   (design / modern buildings)

2. Picasso was a talented artist because he _____

   (paint / in an original way)

3. Women appreciated Maathai's ideas because they _____

   (help / their community)

4. The characters in the film were strange because they _____

   (not / understand / real life)

5. People appreciated the writer's stories because she _____

   (describe / characters / in a powerful way)

6. We bought pictures of our favorite paintings because we _____

   (not / take pictures / in the museum)

D. Use the words in the chart to write sentences.

The writer could tell powerful stories.

The artist	could (not)	appreciate the world around him/her
The filmmaker		connect to people
The painter		create beautiful images
The photographer		show history in an interesting way
The writer		tell powerful stories
		make people imagine life differently

Grammar Note

so that

Writers use *so that* to show the purpose of an action. *So that* combines two subject-verb combinations.

> *Mathaai planted trees* **so that** *people had wood for their homes.*
>
> *She helped people* **so that** *they lived better.*

Use *so that* with *could* to explain that an action made something become possible.

> *The artist continued working* **so that he could support his family**.
>
> *The museum bought his paintings* **so that other people could appreciate them**.

GO ONLINE
for more practice

E. Circle the letter of the phrase that best completes each sentence. Then write the correct sentence.

1. The artist explained his painting so that

   a. people saw it.

   b. people appreciated it.

   The artist explained his painting so that people appreciated it.

2. The photographer took black-and-white photographs so that

   a. they looked old.

   b. they were colorful.

   _____

3. The filmmaker studied history so that

   a. his films were strange.

   b. his films were true to life.

   _____

4. The player concentrated on making the goal so that

   a. his team won the game.

   b. his team lost the game.

   _____

5. The city planted trees so that

    a. the streets looked prettier.

    b. the streets looked busier.

_____

6. The engineer designed the building so that

    a. it used more energy.

    b. it saved more energy.

_____

F. Write the letter of the phrase on the right to complete each sentence on the left. Then write the sentences below.

1. __e__ My brother continued working so that

2. _____ My sister went to college so that

3. _____ The government built a museum so that

4. _____ They concentrated on saving the forest so that

5. _____ The writer used a lot of details so that

6. _____ The artist worked outside so that

a. she could study medicine.

b. they could protect the animals.

c. readers could imagine the story better.

d. she could paint the forest.

e. he could support his college education.

f. the community could appreciate beautiful art.

1. My brother continued working so that he could support his college education.

2. _____

3. _____

4. _____

5. _____

6. _____

Chant

GO ONLINE for the Chapter 9 Vocabulary & Grammar Chant

Writing Assignment Who is your country proud of?

People can change their countries in important ways. Who is an important person from your country? What did he or she do? How did the person affect society?

Step 1 PREPARE

A. Read the paragraphs. Why did Rodchenko take pictures of Russian cities?

Alexander Rodchenko

Alexander Rodchenko was a talented Russian photographer. He took black-and-white pictures of city landmarks, but he saw them differently. He liked sitting on the sidewalk and facing his camera up so that the buildings looked strange. He wanted his photographs to surprise people.

Rodchenko's photographs made Russians look at their society in an original way. He believed that new technology could improve their lives. He also wanted Russian people to appreciate their modern history so that they concentrated on the future and not the past. Today, his images of Russian cities are in famous museums all around the world.

B. Answer the questions about the paragraphs in Activity A.

Paragraph 1: *Who was Rodchenko?*

1. Who was Alexander Rodchenko? _____

2. What did he take pictures of? _____

3. Why were his photographs original? _____

Paragraph 2: *How did Rodchenko affect society?*

4. What is the writer's transition sentence? _____

5. What did Rodchenko believe? _____

6. What is the writer's concluding sentence? _____

A. Look at the list of topics below. Write down people your country is proud of. Then check (✓) one person to write about.

	1. a photographer	Alexander Rodchenko
	2. a painter	
	3. a writer	
	4. a musician	
	5. an engineer	
	6. a sports team	
	7. _____ (other)	

B. Write a topic sentence and a transition sentence. Complete one of the sentences below or write your own sentences.

Topic sentence	Transition sentence
… was a famous… … is a talented… … helped my country.	… makes my country proud. … made people look at… differently. … affected society because…

C. Complete the chart with ideas for the different parts of your paragraphs.

What is the person famous for?   What did the person do? What did he or she concentrate on?
What did the person believe?   How did he or she affect your society or culture?

Step 3 WRITE

A. Organize your paragraphs. Use your Prewrite notes to write sentences.

Paragraph 1: *Who is the person?*

1. What is your topic sentence? _____

2. What details from Prewrite do you want to include?

_____

_____

Paragraph 2: *How did the person affect society?*

3. What is your transition sentence? _____

4. What details from Prewrite do you want to include?

_____

_____

5. What is your concluding sentence? _____

 B. Use your sentences from Activity A to write two paragraphs. Add a title to your paragraphs.

Step 4 REVISE

A. Read the paragraphs. What was Miyazaki's goal?

Hayao Miyazaki

Hayao Miyazaki is a famous Japanese filmmaker. When he made films, he created imaginary characters and strange places, but they still felt Japanese. His films also told powerful stories about intelligent children, independent women, and loving families. He could make people see, feel, and understand the characters' lives.

Miyazaki's films make the people of Japan proud. His films show beautiful images of Japan's cultural history. His films also make Japanese people appreciate their country's natural forests and mountains so that they continue protecting them. Miyazaki stopped making films in 2013, but his imagination will always give Japan an important gift.

Word Partners

make money

make films

make people proud

make people see (something)

make people understand

GO ONLINE
to practice
word partners

B. Read the paragraphs in Activity A again. Circle *also*.

Writing Strategy

also

Writers use *also* when they give additional information about a topic.

first idea about his films	**additional idea about his films**

*His films show beautiful images of Japan's cultural history. His films **also** make Japanese people appreciate their country's natural forests and mountains.*

Use *also* before a verb.

*Rodchenko wanted to take interesting photographs. He **also** wanted Russians to appreciate their modern history.*

Use *also* after the verb *be*.

*Miyazaki was a filmmaker, but he was **also** an artist.*

GO ONLINE
for more practice

C. Write a supporting sentence with *also* and the words in parentheses.

1. Miyazaki was a filmmaker. (was / an artist)

He was also an artist.
_____

2. David Beckham likes soccer. (likes / fashion)

_____

3. She was intelligent. (was / creative)

_____

4. His paintings were colorful. (had / a lot of interesting details)

_____

5. The museum brought a lot of tourists. (improved / the economy)

_____

6. My country is proud of its sports teams. (is / proud of its artists)

_____

D. Rewrite your paragraphs from page 128. Use the questions below to help you.

Oxford 2000 🔑

Do you need more words to write about the person your country is proud of? Use the Oxford 2000 list on page 133 to find more words for your sentences.

Revising Questions

Can you:

- use *also* when you introduce new information?

- use the Oxford 2000 to add more vocabulary words?

- add details?

Step 5 EDIT

Writing Strategy

Verbs followed by gerunds
Verbs such as *continue, imagine, like, prefer, start,* and *stop* can be followed by gerunds.

> The painter **continued working** from her home.
> They could not **imagine growing** trees by themselves.
> She **liked helping** people.
> He **preferred writing** stories for children.
> Buildings **started becoming** tall and modern.
> Miyazaki **stopped making** films in 2013.

GO ONLINE
for more
practice

A. Read each sentence. Fill in the blank with a phrase from the box.

~~continue working~~	like giving	started playing
imagined traveling	preferred living	stopped taking

1. Countries _____*continue working*_____ on better solutions for the environment.

2. The artist _____ in a quiet community.

3. The children in the film _____ to a strange world.

4. David Beckham _____ soccer for England.

5. Many famous people _____ money to people in need.

6. He _____ photographs when he was older.

B. Read the paragraphs below. Find and correct eight mistakes. The first mistake is corrected for you.

My Independent Grandmother

My grandmother worked hard to ~~made~~ *make* her children successful. When there were not enough money to send her son to university, she decided to work so that she can pay for his education. She also wanted her daughter to have a career. When she was studying to be an engineer, my grandmother never stopped support her.

I am proud of my grandmother. When she was a young mother, many women could not worked. Society expected them to stay home, but women like my grandmother not believe this. They preferred be independent, and they continued working so that they could made their children's future better. They were not famous, but they made their country stronger.

C. Read your paragraphs again. Check (✓) the things in your paragraphs.

Editing Checklist

○ 1. Capital letters   ○ 2. *so that*

○ 3. Periods   ○ 4. *also*

○ 5. *could (not)* + verb   ○ 6. Verbs followed by gerunds

D. Now write your final paragraphs. Use the Editing Checklist to help you.

Step 6 PUBLISH

Follow these steps to publish your paragraphs.

Publishing Steps

- Share your paragraphs with a partner.
- Answer the questions
  - What did you learn from the paragraphs?
  - What information surprised you?
- Put your paragraphs in your portfolio!

Critical Thinking Question

Why do countries need creative people?

Extend Your Skills

Look at the word bank for Unit 3. Check (✓) the words you know. Circle the words you want to learn better.

OXFORD 2000 ✛

Adjectives	Nouns				Verbs
black	artist	film		problem	achieve
free	career	future		science	appreciate
less	century	goal		secret	believe (in)
medical	challenge	image		solution	communicate
more	character	job		support	concentrate (on)
original	college	motorcycle		team	continue
powerful	decision	museum		text	create
pretty	degree	opportunity		time	design
real	education	person		way	face
successful	experience	photograph		world	hope (to)
various	farm				prefer (to)
white					protect
					provide
					solve

PRACTICE WITH THE OXFORD 2000 ✛

A. Use the words in the chart. Match adjectives with nouns.

1. ____original solution____   2. _____   3. _____

4. _____   5. _____   6. _____

B. Use the words in the chart. Match verbs with nouns.

1. ____design images____   2. _____   3. _____

4. _____   5. _____   6. _____

C. Use the words in the chart. Match verbs with adjective noun partners.

1. ____provide more opportunities____   2. _____   3. _____

4. _____   5. _____   6. _____

THE OXFORD 2000 ✐ LIST OF KEYWORDS

This is a list of the 2000 most important and useful words to learn at this stage in your language learning. These words have been carefully chosen by a group of language experts and experienced teachers, who have judged the words to be important and useful for three reasons.

- Words that are used very **frequently** (= very often) in English are included in this list. Frequency information has been gathered from the American English section of the Oxford English Corpus, which is a collection of written and spoken texts containing over 2 billion words.

- The keywords are frequent across a **range** of different types of text. This means that the keywords are often used in a variety of contexts, not just in newspapers or in scientific articles, for example.

- The list includes some important words which are very **familiar** to most users of English, even though they are not used very frequently. These include, for example, words which are useful for explaining what you mean when you do not know the exact word for something.

Names of people, places, etc. beginning with a capital letter are not included in the list of 2000 keywords. Keywords which are not included in the list are numbers, days of the week, and the months of the year.

A

a, an *indefinite article*
ability *n.*
able *adj.*
about *adv., prep.*
above *prep., adv.*
absolutely *adv.*
academic *adj.*
accept *v.*
acceptable *adj.*
accident *n.*
   by accident
according to *prep.*
account *n.*
accurate *adj.*
accuse *v.*
achieve *v.*
achievement *n.*
acid *n.*
across *adv., prep.*
act *n., v.*
action *n.*
active *adj.*
activity *n.*
actor, actress *n.*
actual *adj.*
actually *adv.*
add *v.*
address *n.*
admire *v.*
admit *v.*
adult *n.*
advanced *adj.*
advantage *n.*
adventure *n.*
advertisement *n.*
advice *n.*

advise *v.*
affect *v.*
afford *v.*
afraid *adj.*
after *prep., conj., adv.*
afternoon *n.*
afterward *adv.*
again *adv.*
against *prep.*
age *n.*
   aged *adj.*
ago *adv.*
agree *v.*
agreement *n.*
ahead *adv.*
aim *n., v.*
air *n.*
airplane *n.*
airport *n.*
alarm *n.*
alcohol *n.*
alcoholic *adj.*
alive *adj.*
all *adj., pron., adv.*
allow *v.*
all right *adj., adv., exclamation*
almost *adv.*
alone *adj., adv.*
along *prep., adv.*
alphabet *n.*
already *adv.*
also *adv.*
although *conj.*
always *adv.*
among *prep.*
amount *n.*

amuse *v.*
analyze *v.*
analysis *n.*
ancient *adj.*
and *conj.*
anger *n.*
angle *n.*
angry *adj.*
animal *n.*
announce *v.*
another *adj., pron.*
answer *n., v.*
any *adj., pron., adv.*
anymore (*also* any more) *adv.*
anyone (*also* anybody) *pron.*
anything *pron.*
anyway *adv.*
anywhere *adv.*
apart *adv.*
apartment *n.*
apparently *adv.*
appear *v.*
appearance *n.*
apple *n.*
apply *v.*
appointment *n.*
appreciate *v.*
appropriate *adj.*
approve *v.*
area *n.*
argue *v.*
argument *n.*
arm *n.*
army *n.*
around *adv., prep.*

arrange *v.*
arrangement *n.*
arrest *v.*
arrive *v.*
arrow *n.*
art *n.*
article *n.*
artificial *adj.*
artist *n.*
artistic *adj.*
as *prep., conj.*
ashamed *adj.*
ask *v.*
asleep *adj.*
at *prep.*
atmosphere *n.*
atom *n.*
attach *v.*
attack *n., v.*
attention *n.*
attitude *n.*
attract *v.*
attractive *adj.*
aunt *n.*
authority *n.*
available *adj.*
average *adj., n.*
avoid *v.*
awake *adj.*
aware *adj.*
away *adv.*

B

baby *n.*
back *n., adj., adv.*
backward *adv.*
bad *adj.*

The Oxford 2000 List of Keywords

badly *adv.*
bag *n.*
bake *v.*
balance *n.*
ball *n.*
band *n.*
bank *n.*
bar *n.*
base *n., v.*
baseball *n.*
basic *adj.*
basis *n.*
bath *n.*
bathroom *n.*
be *v.*
beach *n.*
bear *v.*
beard *n.*
beat *v.*
beautiful *adj.*
beauty *n.*
because *conj.*
become *v.*
bed *n.*
bedroom *n.*
beer *n.*
before *prep., conj., adv.*
begin *v.*
beginning *n.*
behave *v.*
behavior *n.*
behind *prep., adv.*
belief *n.*
believe *v.*
bell *n.*
belong *v.*
below *prep., adv.*
belt *n.*
bend *v.*
benefit *n.*
beside *prep.*
best *adj., adv., n.*
better *adj., adv.*
between *prep., adv.*
beyond *prep., adv.*
bicycle *n.*
big *adj.*
bill *n.*
bird *n.*
birth *n.*
birthday *n.*
bite *v.*
bitter *adj.*
black *adj.*
blame *v.*
block *n.*
blood *n.*
blow *v., n.*
blue *adj., n.*

board *n.*
boat *n.*
body *n.*
boil *v.*
bomb *n., v.*
bone *n.*
book *n.*
boot *n.*
border *n.*
bored *adj.*
boring *adj.*
born: be born *v.*
borrow *v.*
boss *n.*
both *adj., pron.*
bother *v.*
bottle *n.*
bottom *n.*
bowl *n.*
box *n.*
boy *n.*
boyfriend *n.*
brain *n.*
branch *n.*
brave *adj.*
bread *n.*
break *v.*
breakfast *n.*
breath *n.*
breathe *v.*
brick *n.*
bridge *n.*
brief *adj.*
bright *adj.*
bring *v.*
broken *adj.*
brother *n.*
brown *adj., n.*
brush *n., v.*
bubble *n.*
build *v.*
building *n.*
bullet *n.*
burn *v.*
burst *v.*
bury *v.*
bus *n.*
bush *n.*
business *n.*
busy *adj.*
but *conj.*
butter *n.*
button *n.*
buy *v.*
by *prep.*
bye *exclamation*

C

cabinet *n.*

cake *n.*
calculate *v.*
call *v., n.*
calm *adj.*
camera *n.*
camp *n., v.*
can *modal v., n.*
cancel *v.*
candy *n.*
capable *adj.*
capital *n.*
car *n.*
card *n.*
care *n., v.*
   take care of
   care for
career *n.*
careful *adj.*
carefully *adv.*
careless *adj.*
carelessly *adv.*
carry *v.*
case *n.*
   in case (of)
cash *n.*
cat *n.*
catch *v.*
cause *n., v.*
CD *n.*
ceiling *n.*
celebrate *v.*
cell *n.*
cell phone *n.*
cent *n.*
center *n.*
centimeter *n.*
central *adj.*
century *n.*
ceremony *n.*
certain *adj.*
certainly *adv.*
chain *n., v.*
chair *n.*
challenge *n.*
chance *n.*
change *v., n.*
character *n.*
characteristic *n.*
charge *n., v.*
charity *n.*
chase *v., n.*
cheap *adj.*
cheat *v.*
check *v., n.*
cheek *n.*
cheese *n.*
chemical *adj., n.*
chemistry *n.*
chest *n.*

chicken *n.*
chief *adj., n.*
child *n.*
childhood *n.*
chin *n.*
chocolate *n.*
choice *n.*
choose *v.*
church *n.*
cigarette *n.*
circle *n.*
citizen *n.*
city *n.*
class *n.*
clean *adj., v.*
clear *adj., v.*
clearly *adv.*
climate *n.*
climb *v.*
clock *n.*
close /kloʊs/ *adj., adv.*
close /kloʊz/ *v.*
closed *adj.*
cloth *n.*
clothes *n.*
clothing *n.*
cloud *n.*
club *n.*
coast *n.*
coat *n.*
coffee *n.*
coin *n.*
cold *adj., n.*
collect *v.*
collection *n.*
college *n.*
color *n., v.*
column *n.*
combination *n.*
combine *v.*
come *v.*
comfortable *adj.*
command *n.*
comment *n., v.*
common *adj.*
communicate *v.*
communication *n.*
community *n.*
company *n.*
compare *v.*
comparison *n.*
competition *n.*
complain *v.*
complaint *n.*
complete *adj.*
completely *adv.*
complicated *adj.*
computer *n.*
concentrate *v.*

concert *n.*
conclusion *n.*
condition *n.*
confidence *n.*
confident *adj.*
confuse *v.*
confused *adj.*
connect *v.*
connection *n.*
conscious *adj.*
consider *v.*
consist *v.*
constant *adj.*
contact *n., v.*
contain *v.*
container *n.*
continent *n.*
continue *v.*
continuous *adj.*
contract *n.*
contrast *n.*
contribute *v.*
control *n., v.*
convenient *adj.*
conversation *n.*
convince *v.*
cook *v.*
cookie *n.*
cooking *n.*
cool *adj.*
copy *n., v.*
corner *n.*
correct *adj., v.*
correctly *adv.*
cost *n., v.*
cotton *n.*
cough *v.*
could *modal v.*
count *v.*
country *n.*
county *n.*
couple *n.*
course *n.*
   of course
court *n.*
cousin *n.*
cover *v., n.*
covering *n.*
cow *n.*
crack *v.*
crash *n., v.*
crazy *adj.*
cream *n., adj.*
create *v.*
credit card *n.*
crime *n.*
criminal *adj., n.*
crisis *n.*
criticism *n.*

criticize *v.*
cross *v.*
crowd *n.*
cruel *adj.*
crush *v.*
cry *v.*
culture *n.*
cup *n.*
curly *adj.*
curve *n.*
curved *adj.*
custom *n.*
customer *n.*
cut *v., n.*

D
dad *n.*
damage *n., v.*
dance *n., v.*
dancer *n.*
danger *n.*
dangerous *adj.*
dark *adj., n.*
date *n.*
daughter *n.*
day *n.*
dead *adj.*
deal *v.*
dear *adj.*
death *n.*
debt *n.*
decide *v.*
decision *n.*
decorate *v.*
deep *adj.*
deeply *adv.*
defeat *v.*
definite *adj.*
definitely *adv.*
definition *n.*
degree *n.*
deliberately *adv.*
deliver *v.*
demand *n., v.*
dentist *n.*
deny *v.*
department *n.*
depend *v.*
depression *n.*
describe *v.*
description *n.*
desert *n.*
deserve *v.*
design *n., v.*
desk *n.*
despite *prep.*
destroy *v.*
detail *n.*
   in detail

determination *n.*
determined *adj.*
develop *v.*
development *n.*
device *n.*
diagram *n.*
dictionary *n.*
die *v.*
difference *n.*
different *adj.*
difficult *adj.*
difficulty *n.*
dig *v.*
dinner *n.*
direct *adj., adv., v.*
direction *n.*
directly *adv.*
dirt *n.*
dirty *adj.*
disadvantage *n.*
disagree *v.*
disagreement *n.*
disappear *v.*
disappoint *v.*
disaster *n.*
discover *v.*
discuss *v.*
discussion *n.*
disease *n.*
disgusting *adj.*
dish *n.*
dishonest *adj.*
disk *n.*
distance *n.*
distant *adj.*
disturb *v.*
divide *v.*
division *n.*
divorce *n., v.*
do *v., auxiliary v.*
doctor *n.* (*abbr.* Dr.)
document *n.*
dog *n.*
dollar *n.*
door *n.*
dot *n.*
double *adj.*
doubt *n.*
down *adv., prep.*
downstairs *adv., adj.*
downward *adv.*
draw *v.*
drawer *n.*
drawing *n.*
dream *n., v.*
dress *n., v.*
drink *n., v.*
drive *v., n.*
driver *n.*

drop *v., n.*
drug *n.*
dry *adj., v.*
during *prep.*
dust *n.*
duty *n.*
DVD *n.*

E
each *adj., pron.*
each other *pron.*
ear *n.*
early *adj., adv.*
earn *v.*
earth *n.*
easily *adv.*
east *n., adj., adv.*
eastern *adj.*
easy *adj.*
eat *v.*
economic *adj.*
economy *n.*
edge *n.*
educate *v.*
education *n.*
effect *n.*
effort *n.*
e.g. *abbr.*
egg *n.*
either *adj., pron., adv.*
election *n.*
electric *adj.*
electrical *adj.*
electricity *n.*
electronic *adj.*
else *adv.*
e-mail *(also* email*) n., v.*
embarrass *v.*
embarrassed *adj.*
emergency *n.*
emotion *n.*
employ *v.*
employment *n.*
empty *adj.*
encourage *v.*
end *n., v.*
   in the end
enemy *n.*
energy *n.*
engine *n.*
enjoy *v.*
enjoyable *adj.*
enjoyment *n.*
enough *adj., pron., adv.*
enter *v.*
entertain *v.*
entertainment *n.*
enthusiasm *n.*
enthusiastic *adj.*

The Oxford 2000 List of Keywords

entrance *n.*
environment *n.*
equal *adj.*
equipment *n.*
error *n.*
escape *v.*
especially *adv.*
essential *adj.*
etc. *abbr.*
even *adv.*
evening *n.*
event *n.*
ever *adv.*
every *adj.*
everybody *pron.*
everyone *pron.*
everything *pron.*
everywhere *adv.*
evidence *n.*
evil *adj.*
exact *adj.*
exactly *adv.*
exaggerate *v.*
exam *n.*
examination *n.*
examine *v.*
example *n.*
excellent *adj.*
except *prep.*
exchange *v., n.*
excited *adj.*
excitement *n.*
exciting *adj.*
excuse *n., v.*
exercise *n.*
exist *v.*
exit *n.*
expect *v.*
expensive *adj.*
experience *n., v.*
experiment *n.*
expert *n.*
explain *v.*
explanation *n.*
explode *v.*
explore *v.*
explosion *n.*
expression *n.*
extra *adj., adv.*
extreme *adj.*
extremely *adv.*
eye *n.*

F
face *n., v.*
fact *n.*
factory *n.*
fail *v.*
failure *n.*

fair *adj.*
fall *v., n.*
false *adj.*
familiar *adj.*
family *n.*
famous *adj.*
far *adv., adj.*
farm *n.*
farmer *n.*
fashion *n.*
fashionable *adj*
fast *adj., adv.*
fasten *v.*
fat *adj., n.*
father *n.*
fault *n.*
favor *n.*
    in favor
favorite *adj., n.*
fear *n., v.*
feather *n.*
feature *n.*
feed *v.*
feel *v.*
feeling *n.*
female *adj.*
fence *n.*
festival *n.*
few *adj., pron.*
    a few
field *n.*
fight *v., n.*
figure *n.*
file *n.*
fill *v.*
film *n.*
final *adj.*
finally *adv.*
financial *adj.*
find *v.*
    find out sth
fine *adj.*
finger *n.*
finish *v.*
fire *n., v.*
firm *n., adj.*
firmly *adv.*
first *adj., adv., n.*
    at first
fish *n.*
fit *v., adj.*
fix *v.*
fixed *adj.*
flag *n.*
flame *n.*
flash *v.*
flat *adj.*
flavor *n.*
flight *n.*

float *v.*
flood *n.*
floor *n.*
flour *n.*
flow *v.*
flower *n.*
fly *v.*
fold *v.*
follow *v.*
food *n.*
foot *n.*
football *n.*
for *prep.*
force *n., v.*
foreign *adj.*
forest *n.*
forever *adv.*
forget *v.*
forgive *v.*
fork *n.*
form *n., v.*
formal *adj.*
forward *adv.*
frame *n.*
free *adj., v., adv.*
freedom *n.*
freeze *v.*
fresh *adj.*
friend *n.*
friendly *adj.*
friendship *n.*
frighten *v.*
from *prep.*
front *n., adj.*
    in front
frozen *adj.*
fruit *n.*
fry *v.*
fuel *n.*
full *adj.*
fully *adv.*
fun *n., adj.*
funny *adj.*
fur *n.*
furniture *n.*
further *adj. , adv.*
future *n., adj.*

G
gain *v.*
gallon *n.*
game *n.*
garbage *n.*
garden *n.*
gas *n.*
gate *n.*
general *adj.*
    in general
generally *adv.*

generous *adj.*
gentle *adj.*
gently *adv.*
gentleman *n.*
get *v.*
gift *n.*
girl *n.*
girlfriend *n.*
give *v.*
glass *n.*
glasses *n.*
global *adj.*
glove *n.*
go *v.*
goal *n.*
god *n.*
gold *n., adj.*
good *adj., n.*
goodbye *exclamation*
goods *n.*
govern *v.*
government *n.*
grade *n., v.*
grain *n.*
gram *n.*
grammar *n.*
grandchild *n.*
grandfather *n.*
grandmother *n.*
grandparent *n.*
grass *n.*
grateful *adj.*
gray *adj., n.*
great *adj.*
green *adj., n.*
groceries *n.*
ground *n.*
group *n.*
grow *v.*
growth *n.*
guard *n., v.*
guess *v.*
guest *n.*
guide *n.*
guilty *adj.*
gun *n.*

H
habit *n.*
hair *n.*
half *n., adj., pron., adv.*
hall *n.*
hammer *n.*
hand *n.*
handle *v., n.*
hang *v.*
happen *v.*
happiness *n.*
happy *adj.*

hard *adj., adv.*
hardly *adv.*
harm *n., v.*
harmful *adj.*
hat *n.*
hate *v., n.*
have *v.*
    have to *modal v.*
he *pron.*
head *n.*
health *n.*
healthy *adj.*
hear *v.*
heart *n.*
heat *n., v.*
heavy *adj.*
height *n.*
hello *exclamation*
help *v., n.*
helpful *adj.*
her *pron., adj.*
here *adv.*
hers *pron.*
herself *pron.*
hide *v.*
high *adj., adv.*
highly *adv.*
high school *n.*
highway *n.*
hill *n.*
him *pron.*
himself *pron.*
hire *v.*
his *adj., pron.*
history *n.*
hit *v., n.*
hold *v., n.*
hole *n.*
holiday *n.*
home *n., adv..*
honest *adj.*
hook *n.*
hope *v., n.*
horn *n.*
horse *n.*
hospital *n.*
hot *adj.*
hotel *n.*
hour *n.*
house *n.*
how *adv.*
however *adv.*
huge *adj.*
human *adj., n.*
humor *n.*
hungry *adj.*
hunt *v.*
hurry *v., n.*
hurt *v.*

husband *n.*

I

I *pron.*
ice *n.*
idea *n.*
identify *v.*
if *conj.*
ignore *v.*
illegal *adj.*
illegally *adv.*
illness *n.*
image *n.*
imagination *n.*
imagine *v.*
immediate *adj.*
immediately *adv.*
impatient *adj.*
importance *n.*
important *adj.*
impossible *adj.*
impress *v.*
impression *n.*
improve *v.*
improvement *n.*
in *prep., adv.*
inch *n.*
include *v.*
including *prep.*
increase *v., n.*
indeed *adv.*
independent *adj.*
individual *adj.*
industry *n.*
infection *n.*
influence *n.*
inform *v.*
informal *adj.*
information *n.*
injure *v.*
injury *n.*
insect *n.*
inside *prep., adv., n., adj.*
instead *adv., prep.*
instruction *n.*
instrument *n.*
insult *v., n.*
intelligent *adj.*
intend *v.*
intention *n.*
interest *n., v.*
interested *adj.*
interesting *adj.*
international *adj.*
Internet *n.*
interrupt *v.*
interview *n.*
into *prep.*
introduce *v.*

introduction *n.*
invent *v.*
investigate *v.*
invitation *n.*
invite *v.*
involve *v.*
iron *n.*
island *n.*
issue *n.*
it *pron.*
item *n.*
its *adj.*
itself *pron.*

J

jacket *n.*
jeans *n.*
jewelry *n.*
job *n.*
join *v.*
joke *n., v.*
judge *n., v.*
judgment *(also*
    judgement) *n.*
juice *n.*
jump *v.*
just *adv.*

K

keep *v.*
key *n.*
kick *v., n.*
kid *n., v.*
kill *v.*
kilogram *(also* kilo*) n.*
kilometer *n.*
kind *n., adj.*
kindness *n.*
king *n.*
kiss *v., n.*
kitchen *n.*
knee *n.*
knife *n.*
knock *v., n.*
knot *n.*
know *v.*
knowledge *n.*

L

lack *n.*
lady *n.*
lake *n.*
lamp *n.*
land *n., v.*
language *n.*
large *adj.*
last *adj., adv., n., v.*
late *adj., adv.*
later *adv.*

laugh *v.*
laundry *n.*
law *n.*
lawyer *n.*
lay *v.*
layer *n.*
lazy *adj.*
lead /lid/ *v.*
leader *n.*
leaf *n.*
lean *v.*
learn *v.*
least *adj., pron., adv.*
    at least
leather *n.*
leave *v.*
left *adj., adv., n.*
leg *n.*
legal *adj.*
legally *adv.*
lemon *n.*
lend *v.*
length *n.*
less *adj., pron., adv.*
lesson *n.*
let *v.*
letter *n.*
level *n.*
library *n.*
lid *n.*
lie *v., n.*
life *n.*
lift *v.*
light *n., adj., v.*
lightly *adv.*
like *prep., v., conj.*
likely *adj.*
limit *n., v.*
line *n.*
lip *n.*
liquid *n., adj.*
list *n., v.*
listen *v.*
liter *n.*
literature *n.*
little *adj., pron., adv.*
    a little
live /lɪv/ *v.*
living *adj.*
load *n., v.*
loan *n.*
local *adj.*
lock *v., n.*
lonely *adj.*
long *adj., adv.*
look *v., n.*
loose *adj.*
lose *v.*
loss *n.*

The Oxford 2000 List of Keywords

lost *adj.*
lot *pron., adv.*
  a lot (of)
  lots (of)
loud *adj.*
loudly *adv.*
love *n., v.*
low *adj., adv.*
luck *n.*
lucky *adj.*
lump *n.*
lunch *n.*

M
machine *n.*
magazine *n.*
magic *n., adj.*
mail *n., v.*
main *adj.*
mainly *adv.*
make *v.*
male *adj., n.*
man *n.*
manage *v.*
manager *n.*
many *adj., pron.*
map *n.*
mark *n., v.*
market *n.*
marriage *n.*
married *adj.*
marry *v.*
match *n., v.*
material *n.*
math *n.*
mathematics *n.*
matter *n., v.*
may *modal v.*
maybe *adv.*
me *pron.*
meal *n.*
mean *v.*
meaning *n.*
measure *v., n.*
measurement *n.*
meat *n.*
medical *adj.*
medicine *n.*
medium *adj.*
meet *v.*
meeting *n.*
melt *v.*
member *n.*
memory *n.*
mental *adj.*
mention *v.*
mess *n.*
message *n.*
messy *adj.*

metal *n.*
method *n.*
meter *n.*
middle *n., adj.*
midnight *n.*
might *modal v.*
mile *n.*
milk *n.*
mind *n., v.*
mine *pron.*
minute *n.*
mirror *n.*
Miss *n.*
miss *v.*
missing *adj.*
mistake *n.*
mix *v.*
mixture *n.*
model *n.*
modern *adj.*
mom *n.*
moment *n.*
money *n.*
month *n.*
mood *n.*
moon *n.*
moral *adj.*
morally *adv.*
more *adj., pron., adv.*
morning *n.*
most *adj., pron., adv.*
mostly *adv.*
mother *n.*
motorcycle *n.*
mountain *n.*
mouse *n.*
mouth *n.*
move *v., n.*
movement *n.*
movie *n.*
Mr. *abbr.*
Mrs. *abbr.*
Ms. *abbr.*
much *adj., pron., adv.*
mud *n.*
multiply *v.*
murder *n., v.*
muscle *n.*
museum *n.*
music *n.*
musical *adj.*
musician *n.*
must *modal v.*
my *adj.*
myself *pron.*
mysterious *adj.*

N
nail *n.*

name *n., v.*
narrow *adj.*
nation *n.*
national *adj.*
natural *adj.*
nature *n.*
navy *n.*
near *adj., adv., prep.*
nearby *adj., adv.*
nearly *adv.*
neat *adj.*
neatly *adv.*
necessary *adj.*
neck *n.*
need *v., n.*
needle *n.*
negative *adj.*
neighbor *n.*
neither *adj., pron., adv.*
nerve *n.*
nervous *adj.*
net *n.*
never *adv.*
new *adj.*
news *n.*
newspaper *n.*
next *adj., adv., n.*
nice *adj.*
night *n.*
no *exclamation, adj.*
nobody *pron.*
noise *n.*
noisy *adj.*
noisily *adv.*
none *pron.*
nonsense *n.*
no one *pron.*
nor *conj.*
normal *adj.*
normally *adv.*
north *n., adj., adv.*
northern *adj.*
nose *n.*
not *adv.*
note *n.*
nothing *pron.*
notice *v.*
novel *n.*
now *adv.*
nowhere *adv.*
nuclear *adj.*
number (*abbr.* No., no.) *n.*
nurse *n.*
nut *n.*

O
object *n.*
obtain *v.*
obvious *adj.*

occasion *n.*
occur *v.*
ocean *n.*
o'clock *adv.*
odd *adj.*
of *prep.*
off *adv., prep.*
offense *n.*
offer *v., n.*
office *n.*
officer *n.*
official *adj., n.*
officially *adv.*
often *adv.*
oh *exclamation*
oil *n.*
OK (*also* okay)
  exclamation, adj., adv.
old *adj.*
old-fashioned *adj.*
on *prep., adv.*
once *adv., conj.*
one *number, adj., pron.*
onion *n.*
only *adj., adv.*
onto *prep.*
open *adj., v.*
operate *v.*
operation *n.*
opinion *n.*
opportunity *n.*
opposite *adj., adv., n., prep.*
or *conj.*
orange *n., adj.*
order *n., v.*
ordinary *adj.*
organization *n.*
organize *v.*
organized *adj.*
original *adj., n.*
other *adj., pron.*
otherwise *adv.*
ought to *modal v.*
ounce *n.*
our *adj.*
ours *pron.*
ourselves *pron.*
out *adj., adv.*
out of *prep.*
outside *n., adj., prep., adv.*
oven *n.*
over *adv., prep.*
owe *v.*
own *adj., pron., v.*
owner *n.*

P
pack *v., n.*
package *n.*

page *n.*
pain *n.*
painful *adj.*
paint *n., v.*
painter *n.*
painting *n.*
pair *n.*
pale *adj.*
pan *n.*
pants *n.*
paper *n.*
parent *n.*
park *n., v.*
part *n.*
   take part (in)
particular *adj.*
particularly *adv.*
partly *adv.*
partner *n.*
party *n.*
pass *v.*
passage *n.*
passenger *n.*
passport *n.*
past *adj., n., prep., adv.*
path *n.*
patient *n., adj.*
pattern *n.*
pause *v.*
pay *v., n.*
payment *n.*
peace *n.*
peaceful *adj.*
pen *n.*
pencil *n.*
people *n.*
perfect *adj.*
perform *v.*
performance *n.*
perhaps *adv.*
period *n.*
permanent *adj.*
permission *n.*
person *n.*
personal *adj.*
personality *n.*
persuade *v.*
pet *n.*
phone *n.*
photo *n.*
photograph *n.*
phrase *n.*
physical *adj.*
physically *adv.*
piano *n.*
pick *v.*
   pick sth up
picture *n.*
piece *n.*

pig *n.*
pile *n.*
pilot *n.*
pin *n.*
pink *adj., n.*
pint *n.*
pipe *n.*
place *n., v.*
   take place
plain *adj.*
plan *n., v.*
plane *n.*
planet *n.*
plant *n., v.*
plastic *n.*
plate *n.*
play *v., n.*
player *n.*
pleasant *adj.*
please *exclamation, v.*
pleased *adj.*
pleasure *n.*
plenty *pron.*
pocket *n.*
poem *n.*
poetry *n.*
point *n., v.*
pointed *adj.*
poison *n., v.*
poisonous *adj.*
police *n.*
polite *adj.*
politely *adv.*
political *adj.*
politician *n.*
politics *n.*
pollution *n.*
pool *n.*
poor *adj.*
popular *adj.*
port *n.*
position *n.*
positive *adj.*
possibility *n.*
possible *adj.*
possibly *adv.*
post *n.*
pot *n.*
potato *n.*
pound *n.*
pour *v.*
powder *n.*
power *n.*
powerful *adj.*
practical *adj.*
practice *n., v.*
prayer *n.*
prefer *v.*
pregnant *adj.*

preparation *n.*
prepare *v.*
present *adj., n., v.*
president *n.*
press *n., v.*
pressure *n.*
pretend *v.*
pretty *adv., adj.*
prevent *v.*
previous *adj.*
price *n.*
priest *n.*
principal *n.*
print *v.*
priority *n.*
prison *n.*
prisoner *n.*
private *adj.*
prize *n.*
probable *adj.*
probably *adv.*
problem *n.*
process *n.*
produce *v.*
product *n.*
production *n.*
professional *adj.*
profit *n.*
program *n.*
progress *n.*
project *n.*
promise *v., n.*
pronunciation *n.*
proof *n.*
proper *adj.*
property *n.*
protect *v.*
protection *n.*
protest *n.*
proud *adj.*
prove *v.*
provide *v.*
public *adj., n.*
   publicly *adv.*
publish *v.*
pull *v.*
punish *v.*
punishment *n.*
pure *adj.*
purple *adj., n.*
purpose *n.*
   on purpose
push *v., n.*
put *v.*

Q

quality *n.*
quantity *n.*
quarter *n.*

queen *n.*
question *n., v.*
quick *adj.*
quickly *adv.*
quiet *adj.*
quietly *adv.*
quite *adv.*

R

race *n., v.*
radio *n.*
railroad *n.*
rain *n., v.*
raise *v.*
rare *adj.*
rarely *adv.*
rate *n.*
rather *adv.*
reach *v.*
reaction *n.*
read *v.*
ready *adj.*
real *adj.*
reality *n.*
realize *v.*
really *adv.*
reason *n.*
reasonable *adj.*
receive *v.*
recent *adj.*
recently *adv.*
recognize *v.*
recommend *v.*
record *n., v.*
recover *v.*
red *adj., n.*
reduce *v.*
refer to *v.*
refuse *v.*
region *n.*
regular *adj.*
regularly *adv.*
relation *n.*
relationship *n.*
relax *v.*
relaxed *adj.*
release *v.*
relevant *adj.*
relief *n.*
religion *n.*
religious *adj.*
rely *v.*
remain *v.*
remark *n.*
remember *v.*
remind *v.*
remove *v.*
rent *n., v.*
repair *v., n.*

The Oxford 2000 List of Keywords

repeat *v.*
replace *v.*
reply *n., v.*
report *v., n.*
reporter *n.*
represent *v.*
request *n., v.*
require *v.*
rescue *v.*
research *n., v.*
reservation *n.*
respect *n., v.*
responsibility *n.*
responsible *adj.*
rest *n., v.*
restaurant *n.*
result *n., v.*
return *v., n.*
rice *n.*
rich *adj.*
rid *v.: get rid of*
ride *v., n.*
right *adj., adv., n.*
ring *n., v.*
rise *n., v.*
risk *n., v.*
river *n.*
road *n.*
rob *v.*
rock *n.*
role *n.*
roll *n., v.*
romantic *adj.*
roof *n.*
room *n.*
root *n.*
rope *n.*
rough *adj.*
round *adj.*
route *n.*
row *n.*
royal *adj.*
rub *v.*
rubber *n.*
rude *adj.*
    rudely *adv.*
ruin *v.*
rule *n., v.*
run *v., n.*
rush *v.*

S
sad *adj.*
sadness *n.*
safe *adj.*
safely *adv.*
safety *n.*
sail *v.*
salad *n.*

sale *n.*
salt *n.*
same *adj., pron.*
sand *n.*
satisfaction *n.*
satisfied *adj.*
sauce *n.*
save *v.*
say *v.*
scale *n.*
scare *v.*
scared *adj.*
scary *adj.*
schedule *n.*
school *n.*
science *n.*
scientific *adj.*
scientist *n.*
scissors *n.*
score *n., v.*
scratch *v., n.*
screen *n.*
search *n., v.*
season *n.*
seat *n.*
second *adj., adv., n.*
secret *adj., n.*
secretary *n.*
secretly *adv.*
section *n.*
see *v.*
seed *n.*
seem *v.*
sell *v.*
send *v.*
senior *adj.*
sense *n.*
sensible *adj.*
sensitive *adj.*
sentence n.
separate *adj., v.*
separately *adv.*
series *n.*
serious *adj.*
serve *v.*
service *n.*
set *n., v.*
settle *v.*
several *adj., pron.*
sew *v.*
sex *n.*
sexual *adj.*
shade *n.*
shadow *n.*
shake *v.*
shame *n.*
shape *n., v.*
    shaped *adj.*
share *v., n.*

sharp *adj.*
she *pron.*
sheep *n.*
sheet *n.*
shelf *n.*
shell *n.*
shine *v.*
shiny *adj.*
ship *n.*
shirt *n.*
shock *n., v.*
shoe *n.*
shoot *v.*
shop *v.*
shopping *n.*
short *adj.*
shot *n.*
should *modal v.*
shoulder *n.*
shout *v., n.*
show *v., n.*
shower *n.*
shut *v.*
shy *adj.*
sick *adj.*
side *n.*
sight *n.*
sign *n., v.*
signal *n.*
silence *n.*
silly *adj.*
silver *n., adj.*
similar *adj.*
simple *adj.*
since *prep., conj., adv.*
sing *v.*
singer *n.*
single *adj.*
sink *v.*
sir *n.*
sister *n.*
sit *v.*
situation *n.*
size *n.*
skill *n.*
skin *n.*
skirt *n.*
sky *n.*
sleep *v., n.*
sleeve *n.*
slice *n.*
slide *v.*
slightly *adv.*
slip *v.*
slow *adj.*
slowly *adv.*
small *adj.*
smell *v., n.*
smile *v., n.*

smoke *n., v.*
smooth *adj.*
    smoothly *adv.*
snake *n.*
snow *n., v.*
so *adv., conj.*
soap *n.*
social *adj.*
society *n.*
sock *n.*
soft *adj.*
soil *n.*
soldier *n.*
solid *adj., n.*
solution *n.*
solve *v.*
some *adj., pron.*
somebody *pron.*
somehow *adv.*
someone *pron.*
something *pron.*
sometimes *adv.*
somewhere *adv.*
son *n.*
song *n.*
soon *adv.*
    as soon as
sore *adj.*
sorry *adj.*
sort *n., v.*
sound *n., v.*
soup *n.*
south *n., adj., adv.*
southern *adj.*
space *n.*
speak *v.*
speaker *n.*
special *adj.*
speech *n.*
speed *n.*
spell *v.*
spend *v.*
spice *n.*
spider *n.*
spirit *n.*
spoil *v.*
spoon *n.*
sport *n.*
spot *n.*
spread *v.*
spring *n.*
square *adj., n.*
stage *n.*
stair *n.*
stamp *n.*
stand *v., n.*
standard *n., adj.*
star *n.*
stare *v.*

start *v., n.*
state *n., v.*
statement *n.*
station *n.*
stay *v.*
steady *adj.*
steal *v.*
steam *n.*
step *n., v.*
stick *v., n.*
sticky *adj.*
still *adv., adj.*
stomach *n.*
stone *n.*
stop *v., n.*
store *n., v.*
storm *n.*
story *n.*
stove *n.*
straight *adv., adj.*
strange *adj.*
street *n.*
strength *n.*
stress *n.*
stretch *v.*
strict *adj.*
string *n.*
strong *adj.*
strongly *adv.*
structure *n.*
struggle *v., n.*
student *n.*
study *n., v.*
stuff *n.*
stupid *adj.*
style *n.*
subject *n.*
substance *n.*
succeed *v.*
success *n.*
successful *adj.*
successfully *adv.*
such *adj.*
   such as
suck *v.*
sudden *adj.*
suddenly *adv.*
suffer *v.*
sugar *n.*
suggest *v.*
suggestion *n.*
suit *n.*
suitable *adj.*
sum *n.*
summer *n.*
sun *n.*
supply *n.*
support *n., v.*
suppose *v.*

sure *adj., adv.*
surface *n.*
surprise *n., v.*
surprised *adj.*
surround *v.*
survive *v.*
swallow *v.*
swear *v.*
sweat *n., v.*
sweet *adj.*
swim *v.*
switch *n., v.*
symbol *n.*
system *n.*

T
table *n.*
tail *n.*
take *v.*
talk *v., n.*
tall *adj.*
tape *n.*
task *n.*
taste *n., v.*
tax *n.*
tea *n.*
teach *v.*
teacher *n.*
team *n.*
tear /tɛr/ *v.*
tear /tɪr/ *n.*
technical *adj.*
technology *n.*
telephone *n.*
television *n.*
tell *v.*
temperature *n.*
temporary *adj.*
tend *v.*
terrible *adj.*
test *n., v.*
text *n.*
than *prep., conj.*
thank *v.*
thanks *n.*
thank you *n.*
that *adj., pron., conj.*
the *definite article*
theater *n.*
their *adj.*
theirs *pron.*
them *pron.*
themselves *pron.*
then *adv.*
there *adv.*
therefore *adv.*
they *pron.*
thick *adj.*
thin *adj.*

thing *n.*
think *v.*
thirsty *adj.*
this *adj., pron.*
though *conj., adv.*
thought *n.*
thread *n.*
threat *n.*
threaten *v.*
throat *n.*
through *prep., adv.*
throw *v.*
thumb *n.*
ticket *n.*
tie *v., n.*
tight *adj., adv.*
time *n.*
tire *n.*
tired *adj.*
title *n.*
to *prep., infinitive marker*
today *adv., n.*
toe *n.*
together *adv.*
toilet *n.*
tomato *n.*
tomorrow *adv., n.*
tongue *n.*
tonight *adv., n.*
too *adv.*
tool *n.*
tooth *n.*
top *n., adj.*
topic *n.*
total *adj., n.*
totally *adv.*
touch *v., n.*
tour *n.*
tourist *n.*
toward *prep.*
towel *n.*
town *n.*
toy *n.*
track *n.*
tradition *n.*
traffic *n.*
train *n., v.*
training *n.*
translate *v.*
transparent *adj.*
transportation *n.*
trash *n.*
travel *v., n.*
treat *v.*
treatment *n.*
tree *n.*
trial *n.*
trick *n.*
trip *n., v.*

trouble *n.*
truck *n.*
true *adj.*
trust *n., v.*
truth *n.*
try *v.*
tube *n.*
tune *n.*
tunnel *n.*
turn *v., n.*
TV *n.*
twice *adv.*
twist *v.*
type *n., v.*
typical *adj.*

U
ugly *adj.*
unable *adj.*
uncle *n.*
uncomfortable *adj.*
unconscious *adj.*
under *prep., adv.*
underground *adj., adv.*
understand *v.*
underwater *adj., adv.*
underwear *n.*
unemployment *n.*
unexpected *adj.*
unexpectedly *adv.*
unfair *adj.*
unfortunately *adv.*
unfriendly *adj.*
unhappy *adj.*
uniform *n.*
union *n.*
unit *n.*
universe *n.*
university *n.*
unkind *adj.*
unknown *adj.*
unless *conj.*
unlikely *adj.*
unlucky *adj.*
unpleasant *adj.*
until *conj., prep.*
unusual *adj.*
up *adv., prep.*
upper *adj.*
upset *v., adj.*
upstairs *adv., adj.*
upward *adv.*
urgent *adj.*
us *pron.*
use *v., n.*
used *adj.*
used to *modal v.*
useful *adj.*
user *n.*

The Oxford 2000 List of Keywords

usual *adj.*
usually *adv.*

V

vacation *n.*
valley *n.*
valuable *adj.*
value *n.*
variety *n.*
various *adj.*
vary *v.*
vegetable *n.*
vehicle *n.*
very *adv.*
video *n.*
view *n.*
violence *n.*
violent *adj.*
virtually *adv.*
visit *v., n.*
visitor *n.*
voice *n.*
volume *n.*
vote *n., v.*

W

wait *v.*
wake (up) *v.*
walk *v., n.*
wall *n.*
want *v.*
war *n.*
warm *adj., v.*
warn *v.*
wash *v.*
waste *v., n., adj.*
watch *v., n.*
water *n.*
wave *n., v.*
way *n.*
we *pron.*
weak *adj.*
weakness *n.*
weapon *n.*
wear *v.*
weather *n.*
website *n.*
wedding *n.*
week *n.*
weekend *n.*
weigh *v.*
weight *n.*
welcome *v.*
well *adv., adj., exclamation*
    as well (as)
west *n., adj., adv.*
western *adj.*
wet *adj.*
what *pron., adj.*

whatever *adj., pron., adv.*
wheel *n.*
when *adv., conj.*
whenever *conj.*
where *adv., conj.*
wherever *conj.*
whether *conj.*
which *pron., adj.*
while *conj., n.*
white *adj., n.*
who *pron.*
whoever *pron.*
whole *adj., n.*
whose *adj., pron.*
why *adv.*
wide *adj.*
wife *n.*
wild *adj.*
will *modal v., n.*
win *v.*
wind /wɪnd/ *n.*
window *n.*
wine *n.*
wing *n.*
winner *n.*
winter *n.*
wire *n.*
wish *v., n.*
with *prep.*
within *prep.*
without *prep.*
woman *n.*
wonder *v.*
wonderful *adj.*
wood *n.*
wooden *adj.*
wool *n.*
word *n.*
work *v., n.*
worker *n.*
world *n.*
worried *adj.*
worry *v.*
worse *adj., adv.*
worst *adj., adv., n.*
worth *adj.*
would *modal v.*
wrap *v.*
wrist *n.*
write *v.*
writer *n.*
writing *n.*
wrong *adj., adv.*

Y

yard *n.*
year *n.*
yellow *adj., n.*
yes *exclamation*

yesterday *adv., n.*
yet *adv.*
you *pron.*
young *adj.*
your *adj.*
yours *pron.*
yourself *pron.*
youth *n.*